SCIENCE AND SPIRITUALITY
An Autobiography

About the Author

Prof. J.N. Nanda besides being an "Eminent Scientist" with two earned doctorates in Physics and Applied Physics respectively has also been active in the social and cultural sphere. He was the first scientist in India to begin research work in oceanography and underwater sound. He prefers the advance of co-existence rather than aiming at "unity in diversity". Understanding the complexity of human mind, he advocates a new Mahayana of co-existence and earnest efforts to square beliefs with advances in science and technology. He has numerous papers and books to his name. He has travelled extensively and led some government delegations abroad.

SCIENCE AND SPIRITUALITY

AN AUTOBIOGRAPHY

J.N. NANDA

LOGOS PRESS
NEW DELHI-110002

ISBN-13: 978-81-7268-221-7

First Published 2013

Published and Printed by
LOGOS PRESS
4788-90/23, Ansari Road,
Darya Ganj, New Delhi-110002 (INDIA)
Phone : 23272187
Website: www.logospressindia.com
Email: info@logospressindia.com

Cataloging in Publication Data--*Courtesy:* D.K. Agencies (P) Ltd. <docinfo@dkagencies.com>

Nanda, J. N., 1920-
Science and spirituality : an autobiography / J.N. Nanda.
p. cm.
Includes index.
ISBN 9788172682217

1. Nanda, J. N., 1920- 2. Scientists—India—Biography. 3. Science and spiritualism. I. Title.

DDC 509.2 23

Preface

An observant person will have insights and comments that can be best conveyed to the public in an autobiography. The reader can also assess if the life that was unfolding had been of one who led it and not of one who just experienced it. I was fortunate in having had a very wise mother who could face the world and bring up her five sons when her husband died when I, the youngest was only one year old. She managed the available resources and taught her children the virtues of obedience and love and of the adage "*sarve bhadrani pashyantu*" *i.e.* expect all to be civilized. While writing my life, I have often digressed to comment on matters of particular interest at any given time to India. The world, in the year 1947 when India emerged as free country, was sitting on a cauldron of ethnic and economic conflicts in the shadow of the crouching nuclear weapons.

In 1992, I presented my book on *Conflicts and Co-existence* to Prof. Galbraith at the Harvard University. He suggested that I should write on India's Foreign Policy which I did in 1997 in my book entitled Foreign Policy of Co-existence—India, as well as in the book entitled *Resurgent India* (2011) with my co-author Shri M.S. Batra. In this story of my life, the chapter on Kanpur where I raised my children during their early schooling, I have commented on the India-Pakistan yea and nay affair. India's emergence on the world scene is a stroke for world peace and cooperative progress for the entire mankind. In ancient times, India gave the world the concept of Mahayana or the spacious vehicle of the Hindu-Buddhist canon so that all religions and modes of worship could flourish in peace and work towards moral regeneration.

I gratefully acknowledge the debt I owe my ancestors, my teachers and my friends for the satisfying life I have enjoyed and hope to enjoy for some more time. Dr. M.A. Tuve, the head of DTM (Department of Terrestrial Magnetism), a branch of Carnegie Institution of Washington D.C. (USA) endorsed with confidence my unabating desire to serve science and my country. I remember keenly Dr. S.D. Chatterji of Jadavpur University, who taught me virtues of patience and hard work and was very enthusiastic about my work in oceanography and geophysics. I shall never forget the love and guidance I enjoyed from Dr. P.K. Kichlu, the head of the research wing of the Panjab University Physics department in the Government College, Lahore where I completed my education in Physics and obtained the first Ph.D. degree. I had also the good fortune of being a favourite student of Prof. R.P. Feynman where I attended his courses in Mathematics during my studies for the Ph.D. degree in Applied Physics of the Cornell University. The National Defence College Course in India when they began their first course brought me in touch with the problems faced by newly independent India. My elder brothers who are unfortunately no more never allowed the absence of my father to interfere with my life of study and research. One of my brothers, Shri Rajendra was a prominent Congress man of the Punjab who had run a course in History and worldwide revolutionary struggles which was attended by most jailed politicians in the Multan Jail. He had worked as one from Punjab Congress in the Mahatma Gandhi camp at Wardha in 1942 and was active in the 1942 struggle.

I acknowledge with fervour the great intelligence and love for righteousness of my wife who unfortunately passed away after severe illness in 2009. My sons and daughter have been of utmost help in promoting my tasks and ideas. My thanks are due to Padma Vibhushan Dr. A.R. Kidwai who extended his brotherly affection to me ever since we met in 1946. He is also the chairman of the Zaheer Science Foundation (ZSF) at Delhi in which I have now the responsibility as Director (Post Graduate Science Education).

The autobiography is profusely illustrated with photographs of family members and friends, etc.

New Delhi
March 27, 2011

J.N. NANDA

Contents

List of Photographs

I

Introduction

India had succumbed to British domination by the middle of the nineteenth century. The political organization based on kingship is extremely precarious for succession of one king by another. The dynastic troubles and occasional bouts of misrule raise strife and rebellion. In such conditions, western trading companies dedicated to profit behind a smoke-screen of neutrality benefited by offering help at a price. The insidious expansion of company rule was first opposed by a mutiny in the mercenary Indian troops of the Company which soon swelled into a spontaneous first war of independence with feudal leadership dreaming of restoration of various feudal rights. This mutiny and struggle was ruthlessly crushed. The rule passed directly to the government in London with each district having a British officer in control. Large parts still made a kaleidoscope of states ruled by hereditary princes under the shadow of British officers as agents. The princes held to their symbols of royalty at the mercy of the British overlords who solved their succession problems, guaranteed their state borders against encroachment by neighbours or against rebellion of their subjects. Still many princely states were continuously diminished territorially as well as deprived of wealth which was spent on empty displays and not on the future of the states. The permanent settlement entrenched the defeated aristocracy in the art of exploiting the villages for themselves or the overlords.

Under the plea of neutrality in Indian religious affairs, the religious management had no control and inputs from the government and merrily decayed into sloth and vice. This official neutrality has still continued to the detriment of true religion in each calling because of the communal virus so diligently pampered by the imperial government. This now is entering caste calculations. The priestly class which is mostly isolated from world developments, is turning fundamentalist in order to impress the laity by their enthusiasm for outmoded communal slogans. Even in the nineteenth century, India had considerable academic, literary and technological capabilities, but why would the alien government build on the Indian system. They were only interested in necessary and sufficient capability with the Indians to help them run the country and exploit it by their clerical and routine assistance. Indians were told to communicate in English and English was made the medium of instruction. Till to-day an Indian child has to spend major learning time up to the university degree for mastery of the English language. Our knowledge of science, technology, management, and medicine, therefore, suffers. The job of doing away with English medium is becoming more difficult because all teachers and textbooks only exist for education in the English medium. An effort is to begin teaching diploma level science, etc., for the training of myriads of technicians and health workers that we need, using their elementary school language laced with technical words from the English language and appropriating the Roman script for this exercise. Slowly advanced textbooks and teachers using the new Indian languages (in Roman script) should become available but alas. This has not happened.

The European trading companies came to the east in search of goods, at bargain prices, for which markets in Europe were clamouring. Soon when the profits had been invested in the industrial revolution, they were on the lookout for captive markets in the east for their mass produced industrial goods. In the beginning of the twentieth century, even hairpins and match-sticks, sanitaryware or drainage pipes were being imported from England. First challenge to the British Empire came from Germany, another ambitious nation of Europe and the empire was shaken to its roots by the first world war, in order to win which, defence and communication industries were started in India along with promises of political reform leading to dominion status. Simultaneously new policies of attaching political significance to communal labels were let loose. Although the British led Indian army loyally assisted the British in many theatres of war, the repression at the end of the war, with the victory of the allies, even disillusioned the moderates including Mahatma Gandhi who had fully endorsed the war effort placing faith in the promises in spite of his experience of such promises in South Africa.

A sense of jolt was experienced by the Muslims in India since they had hoped that from their contribution to the allied war effort, the Caliphate would be preserved. But even the Turks disowned the Caliph, under the leadership of Ataturk. The Muslims had mounted an agitation for the restoration of the Caliph, jointly with the civil disobedience movement under the leadership of Mahatma Gandhi. The movements were suppressed and a royal commission came to India for suggesting reforms. This visit of the commission without any Indian nominated on it caused further unrest.

The country was seething with discontent. In this situation, a trigger happy British official at Amritsar ordered firing on a protest meeting on the Baisakhi day. The massacre at the Jalianwala Bagh brought home to the people their servitude to the British. Political bondage was not the only misfortune. Lack of social justice, caste prejudice, superstition and obsolete values were causing more damage. India had been projecting religious as well as secular reformers, but there was indifference from the state which was happy in further degradation of values. There was in fact only encouragement to an emphasis on separatism. In the Punjab the reformist Arya Samaj movement was growing in popularity. Their innovative plank of reconversion, of those who were willing, to Hinduism was picked up by Muslims as anti-Muslim and situation became ripe for a bout of communal quarrels. The Sikhs were organized into Singh Sabhas with a plank of cleansing the Gurudwaras from Hindu symbols and foundation was laid for the imaginary Hindu-Sikh differences which have borne the evil fruit now when Sikh citizens of U.S.A. and Canada started to give the lead to the millions of Sikhs of India that they were not Hindus. After mutual recrimination, the civil disobedience movement against the British rule fizzled out. The stock derogatory view of the other communities became common currency. Average Muslim regarded the average Hindu as a weakling, a Koranic Kafir to be treated as a sub-human. An average Hindu had a self-image of great piety and tolerance and to him an average Muslim was so unclean that his touch defiled water which became unfit for him and there was the spectacle of government making separate arrangements for drinking water for Hindus and Muslims in public places and railways, (with independence all this has gone.) Mahatma Gandhi was correct in giving the nation a priority programme of Hindu-Muslim unity and the eradication of untouchability. These programmes are still valid. Only they have wider dimension, now we need secularism or communal amity between all the great religions of India. Untouchability is now illegal but the lack of skills and training, hopelessness of backward and depressed classes has resulted in some government job reservations for them which is what we blame the British for doing for Muslims and Sikhs thus giving the difference in religious labels an economic base for becoming entrenched in the country. One can only hope that the general prosperity of the future will submerge these superficial caste privileges and casteism is forgotten. A time limit shall be placed on caste and religion based privileges.

In the aftermath of the Jalianwala Bagh massacre, I was born in 1920 in an average Hindu family of the Punjab. My father, Shri Gauri Shankar Nanda of Batala was a station master in the employment of the North Western Railway. My mother, Shrimati Lakshmi Devi was a devout lady hailing from a Bedi family of Phagwara. Unfortunately my father died when I was one year old. My mother shifted to the ancestral house at Batala where I spent my childhood. The elder two of us, five brothers, went to pursue their higher secondary and engineering diploma courses elsewhere. The local guardian was my brother Kidarnath, himself eight years old. We moved to Lahore only in 1930 to live with the second elder brother.

Mahatma Gandhi had returned from South Africa in 1915. He supported the Champaran Satyagraha in 1916. Later, the repressive Rowlett Act was imposed by the British Parliament. Maulana Azad had presided over the Khilafat Conference in February 1920 for retention of the Muslim Caliph and for better terms for Turkey, but Ataturk and Amanullah had led the people of Turkey and of Afghanistan out of obscurantism. The exploits of Amanullah and the devotion of Baccha Saqa, a water carrier, were on people's mind. It is unfortunate that the people of Afghanistan have succumbed to the machinations of U.S.A., ostentatiously against the Soviet Union but which have deprived them of sane secular polity. The Pathans who had been the worshippers of the Buddha at one time and who had accepted the lead of Abdul Ghaffar Khan, the Frontier Gandhi in non-violence and took valiant part in the freedom struggle have become refugees in their own land. They are branded anti-national by the Pakistan officialdom.

When the civil disobedience movement was withdrawn in 1922 after Chauri Chaura violence, the mutual recrimination led to the first major Hindu-Muslim riots symbolized by Kohat riots of 1924 when the entire Hindu population was thrown out of the town. The leadership of the Congress now gave priority to the regeneration of the people of India through communal amity and vows to buy Indian made goods. Use of home spun khadi and a constructive programme for rural reconstruction became potent weapons to fight the Empire. There were bonfires of imported cloth all over India. I recall the one outside the Teli gate in Batala.

II

Batala

As in any Punjabi family, there was considerable inter-faith philosophy because of the rise of the Sikh faith in the Punjab. My mother being from a Bedi family was a direct descendent from Guru Nanak, the first Guru of the Sikhs. Her father was a Hindu, but the family had built a gurudwara in their street and most of the clan worshipped there. She devotedly recited the Japji Sahib (the Sikh prayer) in the morning, but in the evening she would recite the Arti, the usual Hindu evening prayer. In our house there was a shrine in honour of a Muslim pir (a holy man) and each Thursday evening a lamp was lit there in his honour and sweets distributed to the children who would collect there. On Sundays she would either visit a Hindu temple or a gurudwara or the local Arya Samaj ladies gathering depending on her convenience, but these visits were not a compulsion with her. Even in any temple or before the holy book or an idol, she would never prostrate herself, but only stand for a moment with folded hands, praying I believe for long life and worldly success for her children. I learnt secular respect for all religions at mother's knee.

I liked going to school and be in teacher's good books. Once a school inspector was so impressed with my enthusiasm to give a satisfactory recitation to his exacting standards that he forecast a bright future for me. The school calendar was studded with holidays for various festivals. Now-a-days a festival day means special television programme for viewing at home. In those days a festival meant considerable activity for festival cooking and preparation if one or more members were to participate in the associated street corner or temple stage programme of music, or a dance recital. Sometimes, a festival day meant a day long picnic with mother either in the temple and gardens surrounding the grand tank of water (about a mile in perimeter) or in the mango garden belonging to our family surrounding a public tank and temple of the mother goddess.

Those days were certainly different. Now every alley is full of children playing their games. In my childhood, my brother (two years older than me) and I were hard put to discover similar age group friends. Our beat would be the neighbouring few streets, i.e., about two score houses, to some of which our mother might go for social occasions. Every evening few of us would collect in the tiny neighbouring square to play children's universal games like gulli-danda, races, hide and seek and detection of scribbled and hidden lines, etc. When I was post doctoral research fellow in the States, on my attempt to describe these games and to demonstrate them, I was agreeably surprised to learn that most of my colleagues also had played similar games when they were children, but they regretted that their children no longer enthused on them and preferred to play horse shoes and nine pins. The relatively grown ups there were taken up by more serious games like holding hands or skating. One can hardly compare my life as a child with the life of my grand children growing in the States. They have no friends within walking distance. In order to meet a friend, their mother has to first agree to an appointment, when two friends can meet and play and can be delivered and fetched by car.

My school was couple of kilometres away and small fry had no school playground for any evening sports. The high school students had hockey practice in school playground about a couple of kilometres out of town in a different direction than the school. The town was not planned for child raising. The old town planner was only keen on the town not getting inundated after rains since it was situated in a depression. He had got constructed twelve large tanks surrounding the town and the Hasli stream overflowed out of the town after all the tanks were full to the brim. There was a town wall with half a dozen imposing gates, two of which I often used, one for going to school and one for visits to our garden or the grand tank. This tank was a place worth a visit. On one side were old palaces of the Maharaja Ranjit Singh's resident governor at Batala. These structures now housed an orphanage, usually for the unwanted children of colonial officers and it later developed into a college open to all citizens. There was an ancient pleasure pavilion at the centre of the tank to be reached by boat. One side of the tank had been reserved for washermen and boatmen as well as a pir's tomb. A row of temples existed on another side and the side nearest to the town had separate bathing ghats for men and for women. The women also came there to wash clothes.

It was a period of a dip in the population after the anarchy following the Mughal rule and then after a brief interlude, the anarchy after the Sikh rule. In general the British were accepted as a non-interfering just rulers. I am told that when there was a great railway strike, it did not have much effect in the Punjab and the trains ran there as usual. Talking of playgrounds, one of our rich neighbours who also happened to be a school master (later turned an industrialist) owned a beautiful large walled lawn and garden which he left open for us, the neighbourhood children including a couple from his extended family. We had tireless games of cricket there with a tennis ball and genuine bat but improvised wickets. We were quite fond of spending some vacations in Batala when we had shifted later to the large city of Lahore. Lot of time was spent in serious conversations about the political news since my brother had a zest for news and newspapers. He had a free supply of one Lahore newspaper as a prize for his articles that they sometimes printed.

A fixture in summer was some wandering *sadhu* (religious mendicant) who might decide to spend one or two summer months in the open close to the street square frequented by us. Usually few ladies will be there to listen to the *sadhu's* religious and other lore about his wanderings to places of pilgrimage. Every season there would be few occasions for food for all on behalf of the local rich or the temple or the gurudwara. The ladies would help in the cooking and feeding. Attending various fairs was always enjoyable. The annual Ram Naumi procession with many floats both static and on the move were masterpieces of devotional display. Our street enjoyed the reputation of having one of the two Ram Lila folk enactments of various aspects of the Rama story, which were the talk of the town. The best actor applause would always be reserved for Guruji who acted as Hanuman with great verve and understanding. They actually enacted the burning of Lanka by Hanuman. The static floats were the prerogative of the "untouchables" of the locality. Under the growing influence of the Arya Samaj, our folk gladly took the sweets distributed by the untouchables when they wanted us to show our willingness to let them be our social equals. It is surprising how popular memory first downgrades some historical incidents and then forgets them. Punjab's history is least researched and perhaps holds the key to the ups and downs in the story of the subcontinent. Only the floats put up by the "untouchables" harked on the forgotten chapters of Punjab history of Pooran Bhagat, Raja Rasalu, and Sirkup or Raja Harishchandra. These were famous characters of History before the Mughals and the Sikhs. Some of these characters found an echo in cheap vernacular texts in Punjabi or Urdu but on the partition of the Punjab, the Pakistan side would not care much to perpetuate the memory of these heroes. Even the exploits of Guru Gorakhnath, the most famous Yogi of Pakistan mentioned in Heer Ranjha are not to be seen in print neither in Pakistan nor in India. Same is true regarding the famous secular Muslim hero Doolo Bhatti whose exploits are sung by children even now on the Indian winter festival of Lohri. The school lessons only dealt with the emperors and viceroys at Delhi, but the folk history remembers the *Ramayana* and *Mahabharata* heroes and also the Hindu rulers of Sialkot (now in Pakistan) where the Hindu Shahi rulers of Kabul established themselves with the help of the Hindu kings of Kashmir after the genocide of Hindus in Kabul by the Arab-Iranians after overcoming their long resistance for two centuries. It is not necessary that factions must be at each other's throat. The castes usually coexisted peacefully. We blame factionalism for lack of progress, but half the time the quarrels are created by the enemies who have an axe to grind. India always had religious and caste factions, but the society worked as a whole organism; factions became quarrelsome only by the machinations of the imperialists. Now the blinkers of self-interest and greed are hiding the true path of self-reliance and hard work leading to progress. The Indian leadership has now to reunite the castes and creeds behind a single agenda of national regeneration.

I looked forward to the winter sport of kite flying. I loved to run after the free falling cast away kites. In the Punjab there were two kite flying festivals: one, the Lohri festival in mid-winter and the other on the Basant Panchmi festival day on the advent of spring. The children or the grown-ups who still could enjoy the joys of youthful pastimes fly kites from house-tops or in the fair-grounds. I discovered later that the pastime of kite flying was almost a craze in Gujarat. In one city of Baroda alone the kite flying generates business of few crores of rupees.

The Holi festival in the beginning of summer is entertaining and practically everyone is a fair target for greetings expressed by colour spray. The more one protests, the more he or she will be soaked. People go about in groups to seek their friends and greet them on this day by touch of dry colour at least. In the evenings usually there are other pranks, practical jokes and competition in rhyme making and airing of critical jokes leading to the crowning of an elected fool. All Punjabis are now recalling the value of Holi in cementing the friendly feelings between participants. Many places have Holi revelry for about a week. On the festival day itself, crowds gather at the houses of managers and the influential for exchange of greetings. The atmosphere is like that of Eid Milad, the festival of cheer of the Muslims.

It is right to believe that one is himself the architect of one's future and not a plaything of destiny but it is difficult to say if the future will turn out in detail as planned. Much will depend on one's innate quality of mind and health, i.e., genes inherited from fore-fathers, and also other random happenings and influences. Purposeful effort, however, will not go waste. Where immediate results are incongruous, the mind will still develop in the right direction and bring about equally desirable fruit. There is a firm under-current of Indian belief in the doctrine of rebirth and transmigration of souls. This belief gets a shot in the arm when someone claims to remember bits and pieces of some past life. When science has developed further to be able to understand the working of the human mind, such genuine statements might be explained by other means than rebirth which seems to be farfetched though supported by most religions believing in an after life and accepted by many respected world figures. The Buddha taught through parables on the basis of his past lives. The *yogis* claim that through the practice of easy yogic exercise, one may recall incidents of past lives. It is so difficult often to remember even events of yesterday and one should not be surprised at the loss of memory of past lives. The methodology recommended is to concentrate the mind about past events while keeping a lighted candle in front of one's eyes. The assumption is that the candle will light the obscure corner of the mind where some memories might be lingering. In my youth I experimented on this technique, and repeatedly I saw myself entering as a Christian priest in a church in South America. The scene became so vivid that I was sure, I could recognise the place if I were to reach it by chance. Later when

I became convinced of my deductions that all talk of rebirth and retribution, soul or God might be humbug invented by wiser persons to keep the people on the straight and narrow path of piety. All religious belief is a valiant effort that seems to be insufficient, yet it edges forward the evolution of human civilization. Though the transmigration of souls is difficult to swallow, yet the continuation of the ancestral gene is well established. Even in the present single life, the deeds leave a mark on the mental make-up and influence future decisions. One reaps the fruit of past deeds at least of this life through the imperceptible prior conditioning of one's mind and its capacity (in other words, the *sanskar*) to discriminate and decide among the alternatives that frequently arise. A word of solace is for the pious that in a way the gates of paradise will be kept open for them since there is actually annihilation or real *nirvana* after death. One has to be pious and loving of fellow men for freedom and peace in this life. On reaching these objectives in this life, he need not hanker for another life in this or the other world for a new chance. This is why human incarnation is supposed to be necessary for salvation.

When my mother died in 1944, I was, as would be natural, taken up through grief with the meaninglessness of worldly life and was seriously considering embarking on spiritual quest. Fortunately I had a brief encounter with Prof. Megh Nad Saha who was visiting the Punjab University Physics Department where I was a research scholar. He was convincingly positive that the life of *sanyas*, i.e., renunciation, prayer and meditation is strictly for old people who may be so inclined. For a youngman, doing this would be to run away from the effort and the struggle to enrich human knowledge and growth. Somehow I must have had a guardian angel that protected me from myself getting into some wilderness or the other. About few months earlier I had written to Mahatma Gandhi about my personal feelings on the incarceration and reported mistreatment of my brother in the colonial jails because he had jumped into the affray subsequent to the passing of the Quit India Resolution by the Congress in 1942. (My brother was since 1941, a member of the Sevagram Ashram of Mahatma Gandhi). I now wonder what reply I could be expecting, perhaps a challenge to follow the example set by my brother. But Mahatma Gandhi replied that "one who treads the path of sacrifice, finds his own strength for it". On my return from advanced studies in the United States, I was appointed as a research officer in the Indian Navy with the expectation that I would take over as Scientific Adviser (Navy) after the return to U.K. of a borrowed admiralty scientist. Finding myself back in Delhi in 1951, I was deeply moved by the begging on foot for land for the landless by Shri Vinoba Bhave and his band including Shri Jai Prakash Narain. I thought this could be the priority duty of anyone to follow the footsteps of such leaders in the absence of Mahatma Gandhi, the Christ or the Buddha. I, therefore, sought the two leaders at their temporary camp at the Rajghat to offer to be one of their companions. Both Vinobaji and J.P. dissuaded me with kind words. They pointed out that many can do what they were doing, but I was a specialist expected to give advice and assistance to the Indian Navy at the critical juncture of mounting security crisis of the country. That was the post I must defend than go a begging with them.

Children sometimes mention profundities without realizing what wisdom they may be expressing. A child usually assumes his immediate world to be perfect so long as he has his mother to cling to. Our family house at Batala was a century old 1 1/2 storey construction. The rooms in use were the two fronts rooms on the first floor and a kitchen and store at the back again on the first floor. The ground floor had an entrance, and staircase in front and three rooms at the side and back along with the shrine to the pir Dhol Baba. The ground floor had a covered courtyard with a large sky-light and stairs descending to the basement where in olden days they stored grain/straw or potatoes. The ground floor rooms were all dark and needed lantern for entering and were rarely used except for storing fuelwood or such articles. As mentioned earlier, only on Thursday evenings we assembled there to light the lamp for Dhol Baba. Once when about three years old, I was asked as to what kind of house I shall build when I grew up. I was quite clear that the house we lived in was the best model to copy. I found grave faults in the neighbouring houses while at least some of them were palatial. One house was no good as it was so high that when a puppy fell from the top floor, the poor thing died; another house was inconvenient since it seemed to require too much washing, a third house had too many steps to reach the living area, etc., etc. A special advantage in our house was that one could walk across on the first floor to the neighbour's first floor and meet friends. Architects, please note the requirements of the ones who have to live in the structure.

The load of books that the children have to carry day after day these days to school has to be regarded as a torture of learning that could repel children from books. They naturally would prefer television at home. One can pity the situation when each child is made to carry his own bottle of drinking water to school. One has also to sympathise with innumerable mothers who sweat daily on the home work of the child so that he could keep pace with similarly coached others especially because of the engagement in the English medium when this is not the spoken language at home. When I went to school, none of these problems existed. I began my education in Urdu which is close to Hindustani and Punjabi. We did have to carry a writing board and a primer, but that was all. Home work was not such a fetish. A friend of mine who later became a vice chancellor loves to relate how he carried his cane seat everyday to school so that he could sit comfortably and not in the dust. I liked school especially examinations in which almost invariably I got excellent grades. One of the primary school years I spent with my brother who was an overseer stationed, near the border between the Gujarat district of the Punjab and Mirpur district of the J & K State, on the upper Jhelum canal.

This was a village primary school. In my class III, there were only two students, my brother and I. The total enrolment in five classes was fourteen. A single teacher was supposed to teach all classes. The Maharaja sent prizes each year to all school going children. The head of the village in which the school was situated was known as the *raja*, a Muslim vassal of the ruler of Jammu and Kashmir. Few miles away was the Mangla dam and the temple of Mangla on a towering hill. Besides the canal and associated inspection road and rail track leading to Jhelum, the public communication channel was a track over the hills to Mirpur, the district town of J & K State. After one year, when mother was fully recovered from her illness as she had been under treatment at Patiala where her brother was a medical officer, we could return to Batala for another two years, till Kidarnath would have to enroll in college at Lahore, there being no college education in Batala.

We found that we now had a friend across the street. Majida's father owned a *Dhaba* (a roadside eatery). Majida a child of about ten years age had busy mornings in the *Dhaba*. I do not believe he was going to any school, but he was often available for any games we may think of playing. In the mango season, my brother and I would go on foot to our garden to collect the stipulated two kilos of ripe mangoes every day. Sometimes along with Majida, we went to our tiny farmland where a share cropper eked his living with difficulty. Majida had ebullient spirit. He would lead the group in revolutionary slogans for no rhyme or reason. He knew in detail the whereabouts of most unattended fruit trees in the ruins scattered all over Batala or along public roads. Our outing with Majida was a sort of picnic. History repeated itself, when my children roamed in the grounds of neighbourhood churches in Kanpur for pilfering produce of the fruit trees along with their friend, the son of the watchman.

Later, on account of partition riots and ethnic cleansing of the minorities, Majida with his folk must have migrated to Pakistan. This was in retaliation of the eviction of Hindus and Sikhs from Pakistan. The Batala town was known as Batala the Pious, because of the many Muslim holy men who had in days gone by resided there. One such Shah, the usual calling of a Muslim pir (Shah means king) was a neighbour of ours called Roore Shah. He was a white bearded biblical character with flowing white robes who was also the keeper of a well endowed tomb of some holy man. We sometimes went to see him at his duties with his cronies enjoying some smoke or the other. He had two wives, one was rather old and was the gossip of the locality. On returning from school, if we found mother away for some reason or the other, it was to her that we turned for comfort. It was she who taught me that every time I was to remove my shoes and socks, I must massage my toes to escape trouble later on. I believe this is the best protection against athlete's foot.

The life of the upper caste people was aristocratic, with hereditary attendants doing labour tasks practically at no pay, but only occasional tips and routine gifts of food or cloth each season. Thus the services were available daily of scavenger and water carrier, and every now and then of the barber and of the priest-astrologer. An old Brahmin lady came daily to collect the first baked loaf of bread. This was for the record of the family in heaven. The caste duties have vanished now and everything and more is available by contract for payment. Each sub-locality those days had a washerman and a weaver, but they had no caste compulsion to serve but did normal business in the locality.

III

Lahore

In 1930, since Kidarnath had passed the matriculation examination and the eldest brother wished to support college education for him since already two elder brothers had started earning without college education. Place for higher education in the Punjab was Lahore. We, therefore, moved to Lahore and an added attraction to me was to be with elder brother Baijnath who was a stipendiary student of the diploma course of the McLegan Engineering College at Mogulpura, a suburb of Lahore. It was in Lahore that we were to become intimate with the reform as well as Congress movements.

The world slump of 1930 had ignited rebellion all over Asia. There was the Syan-San rebellion in Burma in 1930-31. Ho Chi Minh formed his party for the liberation of Vietnam while in Hongkong. Bao Dai was made king by the French in 1932. P.N.I was formed in 1927 by Sukarno in Indonesia and a constitutional government was set up in Thailand. The Congress had set complete independence from England as its goal in 1929. The breaking of salt laws was begun, with full intention of extending such activities to other fields, in May 1930. This started the chain reaction that ended with the independence of India and many other colonies of European powers in Asia and Africa. When the Mahatma was in jail, he embarked on a fast unto death to undo the separate electorates for the untouchables or the Scheduled Castes. This shook the Indian society and the politicians to their roots. Harijan uplift became a major plank of the nationalists. The separate electorates were cancelled for them, but their position was otherwise consolidated as reflected later in the Constitution of free India. It was in Lahore that I felt being present at the unfoldment of the struggle for Indian independence. There were frequent public meetings addressed by the Congress leaders. Every now and then there would be an occasion for a mammoth procession. There was picketing on shops selling foreign merchandise, liquor or imported cloth. Every now and then there would be strikes in protest of some arrest or new imposition; and sometimes processions, picketers or mobs would be blocked, ordered to disperse or cane charged by the police. As a child sometimes I watched in the crowd, the arrests of picketers one by one as they came as disciplined non-violent soldiers of the revolution. The Harijan entry into temples became a popular festival in every locality. The upper caste Hindus publicly ate out of the hands of Harijans.

The D.A.V. High School at Lahore to which I was admitted was the largest and quite an independent school in the country. It had been started by donations from the public and the inspiration provided by the first generation Arya Samajists following the teachings of Swami Dayananda. The school refused any grants from the government and could experiment with child education based on ethical values and pragmatic learning of the east and the west. I was indeed fortunate to have studied there. Each class had two to three hundred students split into many sections. This school had a large student library, a gymnasium and a swimming pool. My brother and I remained class fellows and completed our college education at Lahore. After school I opted for science studies and my brother took up study of economics and political science. He became a journalist by profession and later taught journalism at University level. The Congress leaders at Lahore selected him to stay at Gandhiji's Sevagram Ashram for the publication of *Harijan* in Urdu from Lahore.

During the socio-political struggle and possibly, for side-tracking it, there were repeated bouts of communal unrest. Most people were addicted to religion and prayer. They would easily be swayed by rumours of excesses being committed by the muscle men or a mob belonging to one community or the other, especially when the wedge of separate electorates had pried the communities asunder. Sometimes imaginary hurts were invented and agents provocateur were also active since any hotting up of political turmoil ended in sporadic communal tension and riots in some cities. In the Punjab, the government jobs were to be filled in the ratio of sixty-six per cent in favour of the

Muslims since Muslims had not advanced in education. The non-Muslim quota was over full. In fact the recruitment of Hindus to government service came to a standstill. If rarely a job was declared open to non-Muslims, the competition generated was fierce and the net outcome was influence peddling and nepotism. The eldest brother employed in the irrigation department since 1928 was not declared permanent until 1940. His temporary job was extended from year to year, as the permanent positions went first to Muslims. Baijnath who got his diploma at government cost in 1933, was unemployed for couple of years. Accidentally we became neighbours in Lahore of an important Muslim personage of the Data Ganj Bakhsh mausoleum at whose recommendation, he was appointed in the railways as a train examiner. The Sikhs now wanted a job quota to be allotted to them and would not like to be clubbed with the Hindus who usually grabbed most of the non-Muslim quota because of better ability regarding education. This was the start of the estrangement between the two communities that first led to the partition of non-Muslim Punjab into Punjab and Haryana and later gave rise to the slogan of the terrorists that Sikhs were in no way Hindus. The Muslims might have some reason to be estranged from the Hindus who had started food and water discrimination with them. Muslims could not draw water from the same well which was in use by the Hindus and Hindus would not accept cooked food from Muslims. The discrimination was on the way out after Mahatma Gandhi's Hindu-Muslim unity plank and is completely off after independence. But there was never any distinction made with the Sikhs. Hindu-Sikh marriages were not uncommon. The wells and eateries were common. Muslims detested idol worship and were not allowed to enter temples, but Hindus and Sikhs worshipped in common in the same gurudwaras or temples. The amount of skilful mischief that must have gone into the driving of a wedge between Hindus and Sikhs can only be imagined. Secular India has to be on guard to have various communities at peace with each other. The Anandpur Sahib resolution of the Akalis that defined the Sikh identity as non-Hindu was passed in the presence and perhaps advice of an American Sikh who also was a senator in the U.S.A. Later a coterie of educated Sikhs compiling a dictionary of the Punjabi language gave the meaning 'sword' to the Punjabi word 'Bhagwati' written in Urdu and pronounced in Punjabi as Bhagoti. This was entirely a mischief. The Sikh prayer as finalized in Guru Govind Singh's time attached the true meaning to the word Bhagoti before that of Nanak, thus giving the normal precedence to mother goddess before the human preceptor. It is well known that the famous Guru was a devotee, since his remembered previous birth, of the goddess. By cleverly displacing God by sword, the separatists among the Sikhs wanted to remove an obvious link with the Hindu origin and fervour of the Sikhs. On declaring the holy war on the Mughals, Guru Govind Singh worshipped Bhagwati and then waved his sword declaring that he will henceforward rely on his sword. Similarly Shivaji while fighting the Mughals had named his sword Bhavani which is another name of the mother goddess.

The religion that I imbibed was mostly Sikhism and the stories of the exploits of the Sikh gurus. Guru Nanak was my hero as perhaps of every Punjabee child. My mother and many Hindus believed Guru Nanak to be the incarnation of Rama, the hero of the Ramayana. On most Sundays up to the death of my mother in early 1944, I accompanied her to the gurudwara. The gurudwaras invariably had some idols around them since this was good public relations with the many worshippers who were Hindu. The idol worship was also under attack from another quarter, from the reformist Arya Samaj. The Arya Samaj had done considerable service in the field of education. They were the pioneers in education of girls. But they were critical of every creed excepting their own. They regarded even the special esteem shown to the *Gita* by the Hindus, the *Koran* by the Muslims and the *Granth Sahib* by the Sikhs as forms of idol worship. The majority of Hindus are Sanatanists who allow worship of all kinds and are at home in every creed and religious practice. Having studied in the D.A.V. High School of the Arya Samaj persuasion, I had also learnt to take part as well as lead in their Sunday religious meetings, but I soon became a convinced Sanatanist, who love to install and worship idols, but the basic philosophy is to surrender to God and worship him in any chosen manner, i.e., God could also have a form or be formless for the devotee. Their religion is all inclusive and is close to multi-religious secularism, which is now-a-days so essential for all nations. In my secularism, a belief in God is also not essential and ethical values and piety are a part of humanism.

My growing years at Lahore were spent in the shadow of political awakening in the country. We shifted to Lahore just after the Congress resolved to set complete independence as the country's goal and after Lala Lajpat Rai's death as a result of blows from police when he led a protest procession that was violently dispersed. I remember joining the huge procession that mourned the death of Jatindernath Das in a jail through his fast unto death for better treatment of political prisoners. (As a result, the lot of political prisoners did improve slightly). Later the educated prisoners could get books from their relatives and friends and could exchange some censored mail. My brother who was in Sevagram in August 1942, took on the work under the leadership of the Congress socialists for spreading the Gandhi message of 'do or die' in the Punjab and the north-west. He was imprisoned for two years and later was under house arrest at Batala. In prison he ran a study circle for fellow political prisoners and the Congress leaders of the Punjab held him in great respect. After independence, he was appointed as a Public Relations Officer of the elected Punjab Government.

The annual session of the Arya Samaj was an important event at Lahore and a great draw. I was every year engaged in the decoration of the school by writing in paint, slogans and phrases in Hindi, Sanskrit or English under the guidance of the teacher. Processions, strikes and picketing were common. I saw the rise of the Muslim League from arguments in press to a mass movement of the Muslims for violently establishing a home-land for Muslims of India. When the Congress leaders talked about the Muslim demand for partition of the country, they as well as Mr. Jinnah or other Muslim League leaders understood a partition of the country where each part will be a democracy, only in one, the Muslims will be in majority and in the other, the Hindus. This was a deliberate false idea given to the Congress by the League as well as the British. This was the reason that the nationalist press argued vehemently that partition will not solve any problem which could not be solved in the whole country. But the real purpose of the League became clear later when they set about the ethnic cleansing of the areas set for the creation of Pakistan and created equally absurd conditions in the rest of the country when as an experiment a joint Congress and League ministry tried to administer the whole country in 1946. The Urdu word Pakistan means the land that has been ethnically cleansed. This is still their agenda and the small minority of non-Muslims that still reside in Pakistan are only marking time till they are pushed out as was happening in repeated expulsions in the eastern wing till the liberation of Bangladesh since the more cultured Bangladeshis objected to the terror tactics governing their land.

Almost right close to partition, in the Punjab and indeed in the entire land-mass now Pakistan, the Muslim League had no political clout. In Sind and the Frontier Province there were Congress Ministries. In the Punjab there was a government of a political party of Hindu and Muslim Jats. In Kashmir, the political liberation was being pressed forward by Sheikh Abdullah under the patronage of States Peoples Congress. Suddenly because of the opposition of the Congress to Britain's declaration of India's joining the allies against the Axis powers and consequent silencing of the Congress and incarceration of Congressmen, the propaganda of Muslims in danger supported by the ideological underpinning of the Communists, the seeds of partition of India were sown and nourished diligently by the reactionaries and empire lovers of all hues. On the failure of the experiment of sharing of power at the centre by the Congress and the League, the partition became a certainty.

The political struggle had proceeded on the predictable course of agitation, repression, truce, reforms, disillusionment, fasts of Gandhi, to the provincial autonomy in 1937. It was followed by the League drive to wean away the Muslims from the Congress. When the Congress provincial governments resigned on account of differences with the imperial government, the League celebrated the occasion as a day of deliverance. This was followed by repression of the nationalists by the rulers with Muslim League and the Communists as partners. The Quit India Movement, the efforts of the INA and the emerging slogans worldwide of democracy and freedom, caused the people of Great Britain to pause and rely once more on the hand of friendship extended by Nehru in the event of freedom of India. But the effort to build a united India failed with the League's direct action unleashing communal riots all over the country in the later half of 1946. Thus two independent dominions were formed in 1947 with the dagger of future conflict still in the air. India adopted a democratic constitution guaranteeing equal rights to all its citizens with special safeguards for the Scheduled Castes and Tribes.

On the other hand Pakistan was declared a sovereign Islamic state created as a homeland for Muslims of India. Non-Muslims would have second class citizenship. They had already been driven out of most of Pakistani Punjab and adjoining areas. With the connivance of the colonial establishment, half of Jammu and Kashmir areas had been annexed as Pakistan's northern areas and some districts snatched later by force from that State to form Pakistan occupied Azad Kashmir. Along with the repression of the Hindus in East Pakistan, the Bengali language was sought to be repressed there which led to the revolt and eventual break up of eastern Muslim homeland part of Pakistan to became free Bangladesh.

Later in order to convince the Muslims that Pakistan was an Islamic state, unlike most Muslim nations, Pakistan has imposed the ancient Islamic law as the overriding law of the land with barbaric customs of polygamy, inheritance laws discriminating against girls, veils for women and easy one-sided divorce by the husband. The Muslim religion forbids charging of interest and they are finding new euphemisms for it. Apart from their archaic notions about idol worship the main objection to any other religion is the firm Muslim contention that the Koran is the final word in religion and there can be no new religious teaching from the Most High. I am sure that inspite of the immense wisdom of the founders of all religions and their direct access to God, or the holy spirit or the inner voice, they could not have caught all the fish of ideas and morality in the ocean of inspiration. In different climes, different environment, with new tools of intuition and logic, philosophy and religion will continue to reveal new features of the face of truth which could be still hidden. I am reminded of the thinking of a small American child when he stopped me on the street on a Saturday evening and advised that I should not go fishing next day since he and his pa had caught all the fish that morning.

Partition of nations was the pet idea of victorious allies dictated partly by the dying imperialism with an eye on future client states in the event of the next worldwide confrontation. Korea was partitioned and they still do not know how to reunite though both sides claim to be keen on it. Germany was partitioned, but it came together as if a corner brick had been displaced from the Soviet edifice which collapsed soon after. Namibia was separated from South Africa and after it gained democratic freedom, the edifice of apartheid started crumbling. Vietnam was partitioned to the sad disillusionment of the French imperialists and then the Americans. Taiwan is still a second China which the Chinese have sworn to reunite. When India and Pakistan begin pulling together that will be the real demise of imperialism whether of the colonial or the economic variety. The United Nations would have become stronger with an international armed force at its call stationed in selected cantonments throughout the world.

Lahore was the most advanced centre for education in northern India those days. All along the Mall from the University and the Government College at one end, and the Lawrence garden at the other extremity near the canal, there were imposing buildings on both sides. The well known Anarkali bazar and McLeod Road crossed it close to the two ends. The High Court building at Lahore was considered as one of the best colonial structures in the country matched perhaps by the agricultural college building at Kanpur and the Forest Research Institute at Dehradun. Ancient monuments included the fort that housed some memorabilia of Maharaja Ranjit Singh, Shahi Mosque in front of the fort along with the Darbar Sahib gurudwara commemorating the martyrdom of Guru Arjun Dev. Beyond the river Ravi was situated the beautiful tomb of Jehangir amidst a spacious garden and the plain tomb of Noor Jehan. A place was marked near the Shalimar Garden as the *samadhi* of Haqiqat Rai supposed to have been martyred by the fanatic Islamic law as one speaking disrespectfully of the prophet or his kin. The tragedy was in the fact that this was a Hindu school boy who had exchange of hot words with a Muslim class fellow. It is now understood that the memorial mark has been obliterated from the site by the Muslims of Pakistan explaining that it reminded them of a blur on the fair name of Islam even if some misguided Islamic Court might have meted out the death penalty and in addition the records have not been ever unearthed for such an event in the seventeenth century. The citizens of Lahore used to hold the kite flying spring festival there, perhaps they still do so.

Lahore was the city of fashions and fashions began in Lahore and later spread to Calcutta, Bombay and Delhi. Lahore was also the centre of activities of many reformist and socio-political organizations for the Punjab. I have already mentioned the Arya Samaj with imposing centres at Gurudut Bhavan and two other sites in the city.

The Congressmen concentrated at Lajpat Rai Hall and its surrounding structures. The revolutionaries were to be met at Bradlaugh Hall. There were half a dozen colleges affiliated to the Punjab University and all kinds of political and technical institutions of higher learning. I had opted for Science education and studied at the University Physics department for my advanced degrees and a doctorate in Physics. Dr. P.K. Kichlu, my research supervisor was my role model for hard work and objectivity up to his passing away in late seventies. With my brother, an officer of the railway, I visited Quetta, Sukkur, Kotri and Karachi, where I walked on the sea shore for the first time. Compared to Lahore there was little bustle in Karachi. It was a relatively smaller place. I had an interesting visit to Peshawar where I attended the marriage of a cousin as his father was posted near there in the Army Medical Service of the Patiala state forces which along with the army of the Nizam was carrying out the duties of the occupying force in lieu of regular British Indian troops which had been shipped abroad for fighting the axis powers. From there I went twice to the famous Sikh shrine of Panja Sahib near Hasan Abdal to the east of Peshawar and also touched the Khyber pass travelling with uncle in a jeep. My uncle assured me that both the Indian military outposts and the private tribal ones keep good lookout along the route watching that the other side may not make any surprise move to control more area than what they already control. The scenario was like the tenuous control on the borders of the white domain over the American Indian territories westwards of the settled areas. This also reminded one of the intrepid generals Hari Singh Nalwa and Moolraj of Multan during the rise of the Sikh power in the Punjab, who subdued the turbulent Pathans right up to Kabul.

My uncle explained that in reality people of India and Afghanistan were one people. The northern boundary of the Indian subcontinent were delineated by the heights of the Himalayas and the Hindu Kush mountains. (Kush means mountain in ancient Persian). The elements of Hinduism which were truly indigenous were the worship of Shiva as the supremo, continuation of the human race in the form of ancestor worship or worship of the mother goddess in various forms, besides self-mortification and non-violence of the Jains whose philosophy was formulated at about the time of the Vedas. The worship of Vishnu (a form of Sun worship) entered from Afghanistan. The ancient thinkers of Punjab, Kashmir and Afghanistan coloured all Indian religious beliefs. Even after the rise of Islam, the orthodox Muslim divines of Afghanistan became the preceptors of the new aristocracy of India, and some of them lie buried in and around Basi Pathana near Chandigarh which is a place of pilgrimage for the Afghans. The Sufi teachers from the west Asian countries became the treasured godmen for the new Muslims of India. Both Hindus and Muslims of India still revere their tombs in the same way as they would respect the Buddhist relics and *stupas*.

I had often spent some summer vacations in the Gujarat district of the Punjab now in Pakistan where the Muslims were in great majority. The Pabbi hills extend north-south in the middle of the district; the people are poor raising some sheep and cattle and a single harvest in the year. In and around 1935, common folk had no idea about the size of India or the life of people in the rest of the country. They were totally surprised to learn that at one time most people of that area were Buddhists and worshipped the idols of the Buddha. The folk history only talked of Sikander, Rustum, and Amanullah. They agreed that one reaps what one sows, but faith in the Prophet will ensure them a berth in heaven.

Around the beginning of the World War, the crisis deepened in the states ruled by the Indian princes. The British had dangled the independent status for the princes through their treaty rights with them if the British were somehow to leave governing India. No patriotic Indian as well as the princes cared for the partitioning of India into thousand pieces. The pressure on the princes to increase the democratic rights of their subjects and to start democratic institutions in the states grew. Before becoming a college lecturer at Gujranwala, my brother Kidarnath had a spell of service as a teacher in Bilaspur state. Bilaspur is a tiny principality in Himachal Pradesh region. Once he reprimanded a protege (of the Rajah of Bilaspur), who happened to be a student in the school. Kidarnath was told as a favour by the state secretary for education that evening to clear out of the state immediately as the prince's men will put him in the state's jail next morning in view of charges of having been disrespectful to the Rajah. He was later careful not to seek employment in any Indian state. After independence he had also to flee to India and found a lecturer's job in Bhopal. The ruling prince of Bhopal had led many rulers of states for merging their states in the union of India. I have now visited Bhopal many times.

In the winter of 1943, I had to go to Calcutta for using the recording microphotometer in the Science College there as our University Physics department lacked this facility. Calcutta had been under Japanese air attack and it was considered unsafe. Still trains to Calcutta went jam packed and I also stayed there about a month with a class fellow who had become a Naval officer and lived in a large apartment in Hastings. He was at that time unmarried. I went daily by bus and tram to the college and worked in the college. I made friends there with A.K. Saha, the son of Prof. M.N. Saha and Dr. Nag Chaudhuri who was engaged on the construction of the Indian cyclotron there. On the way back from Calcutta I broke my journey at Agra and had my first glimpse of the Taj as in a dream. I went immediately to look at the Taj at about 11 P.M. and there was no moon. But my luck held and I saw the Taj lit up by repeated lightning flashes on account of an approaching winter thunder shower. The view was enchanting and I can recommend such an encounter with the Taj if a tourist can plan an unseasonable visit on a cloudy dark night and camp there. Next day I felt marooned in the crowds at Agra, because railway booking was closed for Lahore on account of heavy rush in trains. Fortunately a policemen who was bringing a prisoner for trial to Lahore from Agra took pity and explained that usually two policemen were required to escort one prisoner, but unfortunately, a second policemen could not be spared. He had a railway warrant for two escorts, and if I were to agree to be his deputy on the journey, he would see that I could travel to Lahore with him. I gladly agreed and completed the thirty hours journey from Agra to Lahore.

I was amazed at the range of my father's scholarship when I could understand the titles in his library. He never had completed even the matriculation examination, but he had mastered many books on English literature and poetry including Shakespeare. His library contained books on law, philosophy, and had some classics of Urdu and Persian poetry. I did not have any benefit of his learning or advice since he died in my infancy. But mother looked after us so well that I never experienced any sense of loss on account of the absence of father in the house. Kidarnath became the responsible man of the house at such an early age. He helped in everyway. He could almost repair and mend everything. He would be in-charge of making home-made soaps, fruit and vegetable preserves under mother's instruction, in order to reduce expenses. My mother managed the sale of garden produce and the small holding of the land given over to a share-cropper. She also had a small earning from giving small loans to the needy neighbours who could be trusted for keeping the agreements with her. There really never was any controversy regarding return of loan with the small interest she charged. She managed her children so well that many neighbours sought her advice on all kinds of problems both while we were at Batala or when we were at Lahore. She once had to correct a white haired neighbour, who wanted her advice concerning the marriage of his daughter and addressed her as mother. She politely told him that he should call her sister and not mother. The Data Ganj Bakhsh Muslim neighbour always treated her as mother and often sought her advice concerning the bringing up of his motherless younger brother. All of us brothers did not pick up any smoking, drinking or any habits she would not approve. At Lahore too, Kidarnath continued to guide us, the younger brothers in our studies and other activities. Baijnath had to observe factory hours and he had to cycle four miles everyday each way to work. He was usually away the whole day except on holidays when he was great company. Often his friends also would spend their week ends at our house since they were almost all of them out of towners. Baijnath was a sports fan especially he was one of the top Punjab (Railways) hockey players. He won many sports prizes. He was the first to display the family characteristic never to accept patronization howsoever unselfish the source. None of my brothers would kowtow to injustice or to officials and often missed the chance of hopping some steps on the professional ladder, being convinced of their merit, recognized or not. He was the natural leader of his subordinates and often got rules reframed when these hurt honest labour of his staff. Labour union leaders were mad at him since his labour would not care to join any union. Once they even demonstrated their anger by injuring him on the roadside at night. He was very fond of acting and staging dramas for the public. Once a play being acted in the Bradlaugh Hall, already noted for revolutionary speeches, so excited the audience, that they started shouting 'long live revolution' at an appropriate scene in the play. The noise attracted the notice of the police ever vigilant at the Bradlaugh Hall. The play was immediately stopped by a police raid and the stage property confiscated. Luckily the cast was not arrested.

During all the while we were at school or college, the slogan was of *swadeshi*, i.e., Indianness of ideas, dress and all purchases. Rajendra was all along engaged on the Gandhian constructive programme and had taken a vow of wearing only khadi which he maintained till his death few years ago. Mother always encouraged him stating that she will want at least one of her sons devoted to the struggle for independence. Had she lived, she would have been very proud to see Rajendra's name engraved on a pillar in Chandigarh as one of Punjab's political sufferers.

When Bhagat Singh and his companions were hanged, the entire nation was stunned, Bhagat Singh's parents and younger brothers and sister had moved to Bradlaugh Hall those days from their village near Lahore. Kultar Singh, the younger brother was our class fellow in school. When grown ups were afraid, we with Kultar Singh and other children established a Bhagat Singh, Rajguru, Sukhdev library at Bradlaugh Hall which functioned for a few years till Kultar Singh left Lahore. After the Congress victory in most State assembly elections in 1937, they formed governments only after receiving an acceptable assurance that the British governors would not override the legitimate decisions of the elected governments. We, Rajendra and I were visiting uncle at Narnaul when the rump government of the Muslim League resigned on the Congress becoming ready to form the government in the Frontier Province where the Congress with the leadership of the Khan brothers had swept the elections. We celebrated the occasion having received a gift money order from Kidarnath, now a lecturer at Gujranwala, for the purpose.

The direct rule of the princes was autocratic but not bureaucratic. The prince exercised complete authority and also delegated it to his appointees fully, within however his final say. The district of Narnaul was cut off from Patiala state proper and had been awarded to the prince for his assistance in the recapture of Delhi during the mutiny. Patiala treated the district as a possession to be enjoyed and had no particular interest in the development of its people or resources. Narnaul was a different world from Lahore. Few hundred metres outside the city one could see droves of deer, a natural threat to farmer's crops, but the peasants could not kill the deer, which belonged naturally to the prince as in England of Robin Hood days. The privileged few of course could hunt the deer at will from jeeps giving no sporting chance to the deer on the run. There was extreme poverty and the district had no decent school. In the Narnaul district as well as in similar areas of Rajputana, there are frequently isolated hills topped by ancient temples or forts. We had an extended picnic to Jaipur for a week with venison ready on the way wherever the private bus used by our family stopped and the state government officials had been alerted to expect us. At one place an expected baghera (a cross between the tiger and the leopard) walked majestically across the road at dusk few tens of yards away from the stopped bus. The poor hunted hedgehogs at night and ate them after roasting on an open fire. Once a local *shikari* (hunter) with a licensed muzzle-loader offered to take us and our cousin brothers on a hunt. We returned footsore after day long chase and stalking of dear and other game with one pheasant as prize. The muzzle loading gun took long to aim and the chosen target got wind of the danger and fled.

During the war years, we experienced the shortages, rationing and high prices, but all attention was focused on the performance of various armies including the Indian National Army, the disclosure of new rockets by Germany and the nuclear bomb by the Americans. The suicide bombing of the British mighty ships by the Japanese and the island hopping campaign of the Americans finally brought the war to a close and once again the attention was back on the success or otherwise of the Indian struggle for independence. The fatigue of the colonial enterprise was visible from one of the incidents that happened in 1944. I was questioned by a British police officer about my views on the Congress struggle when my brother had already been arrested. When I told him that I fully supported the Quit India Movement. To my surprise he made the rejoinder that he will gladly quit the thankless task of governing if only his department would let him go home.

IV

Ithaca U.S.A. (Cornell University)

I was enrolled in the graduate school of the Cornell University at Ithaca in U.S.A. in 1946. When India became independent on August 15, 1947, the Indian flag was placed in the Cosmopolitan Club by the President of the Cornell Hindustan Association. The association undertook to project India across to the university population. We set up the first Gandhi Memorial Library. A comparison with the education in the states made me ponder over the shortcomings in the system prevailing in India. Till now many educationists have prescribed modifications to education in India, but much has yet to be done. Rather than any tinkering with the education system, what we need is an environment of conformity between principles and practice, a strong effort for the spread of the scientific method and a culture of work. Our working year is studded with holidays of all sorts. I was surprised to see home work being given to Ph.D. students and the professors dutifully grading the student papers every week. The education has to be properly stepped up with basic essentials like mathematics and electronics receiving adequate attention for science students. The project system in schools and colleges helps students at all levels in planning, projecting, experimenting and problem solving of all kinds. The teachers put in an enormous amount of labour in U.S.A. There is an interesting description of a professor's life in India of colonial days. We had a laboratory bearer who explained to a friend from his native village that he was then a professor which meant that he came to work at about 11 O'clock when the students had begun their college studies and came for practical work to him. After seeing that they have the necessary apparatus and instruction sheets, he was free and when they left after two hours he had just to put away some of the apparatus.

In the United States of America, especially in a university town there is an atmosphere of honesty and trust. No one seemed to shirk his duties and carried them out without requiring on the spot supervision. There is, however, considerable red tape, but the movement of papers is according to set rules and if a decision can normally be given in a week, this will be done on time. Everyone is keen to make improvements in procedures in order to increase the efficiency for carrying out the real task. The teachers who taught were also the examiners. I never heard even a whisper for having external examiners or that some of the questions happened to be out of the prescribed course. The tests were of the achieved level set by a particular course. There was considerable flexibility in the choice of subjects of study. Besides choosing courses for credit for examination, one could also squeeze in other courses simply for audition thus adding to one's knowledge. At the university it was a veritable feast of knowledge. Besides taking the required courses for credit, I listened to all the courses given in the physics department at graduate level. An average American student has more knowledge in depth in any subject than his counterpart in India. The difference starts from school level. In India half the time at school is spent in learning the English language which alone is the medium of instruction at university level and the teachers and the students have barely the time to learn the story of science or engineering without getting to grips with the fundamentals. The sooner we can replace the English language as the medium of instruction, the better would it be for Indian scholarship. Slowly a workshop language is evolving using the regional language plus technical words borrowed from English and the new language could be written in the Roman script so that foreign words can be lifted bodily. The teaching at diploma level is already going on in this fashion, but the students remain bewildered since the only textbooks that are available are in English and the tests that they have to submit to are also in English. Once the new practical language is recognized by the authorities for technical education, first the textbooks will appear at lower level and later textbooks at advanced level will be available in new Hindustani in the Roman script, and then perhaps the children will be freed from the cramming of English when in the whole world foreign languages are learnt by adults in about six months of special effort.

If there were less emphasis on degrees, perhaps the teachers and the taught can work for knowledge of any subject and problem solving ability. This is feasible in the American system since even if the degree is the culmination of usual residence in the university, the teachers themselves frame the syllabus, give tests to students and evaluate the students themselves. It is the performance of the alumni that places a suitable weight on the education of any specific university. The employers in general can also rely on independent evaluation by special outfits who issue certificates after testing.

I was also very much impressed by the use of summer vacations for university studies. Summer camps and summer schools are held in all universities and institutions so that many can benefit from flexible and piecemeal education by accumulating course credits by separated periods of study. This is a boon for ambitious professionals to give themselves more education. The young students also utilize the vacations for progress in any particular hobby of theirs that can be acquired by stay on a university campus. Many students use vacations for job experience sometimes allied to their subjects of study, sometimes purely for earning and saving for their further education. Most students have to earn or borrow soft educational loans or depend on their steady girl friends who are often keen to invest in the higher education of their chosen friend. The university campus is full of activity and short courses and special courses for teachers, etc. During the academic sessions too, the university has an extension service, i.e., arranging advanced technical training during couple of week-ends and by despatching qualified lecturers to establishments of large employers to give state-of-the-art lectures and demonstrations for key personnel. Many university professors are consultants to industry or defence, etc. They create programmes of research to bear on practical problems. Same kind of faculty-industry interaction takes place in U.K., Germany or Japan. In India this has started now but normally, the institutions in general plough their lonely furrows, while the industry and government merrily import machines and technology. We have exhausted the possibilities of centralized planning and public sector production. Now we are embarking on the failing of the market economy as it failed in the world before the two world wars and in U.K. when they had to nationalize coal and railways. The British are also scrapping the nationalization of railways, why should we be left behind! I hope we stick to our pragmatic policy of going by results and be prepared to give up market economy if the gains are not commensurate with the needs of the times! Any economic theory is only an adjunct to self-help which must remain supreme. We have demonstrated advancement through self-help in nuclear and space technologies.

Prof. D.S. Kothari, the first Chairman of the University Grants Commission of India and the author of the Kothari Committee Report on Education in India, when asked specifically as to the reasons that Indian scientists do less well in India than they do in England or in U.S.A. Prof. Kothari did not agree with the statement. According to him many scientists, e.g., C.V. Raman, M.N. Saha had done their renowned work while engaged on research in India. 1 believe, his mind was still set on the research work of pre-independence days. There would always be an odd genius who will do well in spite of the contrary environment for research of value in the country. The research facility and environment has to be especially better in a developing country trying to lift itself by tugging on its bootstraps. Our planners must face the problem that is very much there. Recently Prof. C.N.R. Rao an eminent Indian scientist lectured on the difficulties faced by an Indian scientist in India. By deliberate pronouncements we have downgraded scientific publications of India, Indian scientific referees, and Indian science planning. The national pastime of backbiting and finding fault with others is very much visible in the scientific field in place of constructive criticism and recognition of new trails. Much of the problem is because the scientific research has become much more costly and dependent on many specialists working towards common goals. With over much accent on individualism and over emphasis on personal competitiveness, cooperation of good scientists suffers. An international journal which was being quoted and abstracted internationally, was closed down in the eleventh year of its publication, because before its start, the institution publishing it did not obtain the permission of the departmental secretary at Delhi. The era of private enterprise and market economy is already limiting government initiatives in the advancement of science while the private capital is not entering research activity or sponsoring quality publications and export of Indian technical books or the expansion of technical training except what is being done by the government.

The American students at the university were a serious lot and engaged themselves also seriously in weekend relaxation. Many youth religious groups were active and were supported impartially by the university chapel and the adviser on student affairs. Once I happened to ask a Chinese student his views on God and Buddhism. This was 1947 when the sway of the Chinese Communists in China was practically complete. He did not think that many Chinese were practising Buddhists. He had great personal regard for Buddha's teaching but belief in God was irrelevant to him or to the Buddha. I became a regular member of the young Quakers and the association was highly rewarding. Sometimes I wandered to the young Jews in their fun on Saturday mornings. The atmosphere among the youths was of serious thinking together with sharing of their joys with others. It was a tension free mixing. The drama club and the glee club often gave free shows and held open rehearsals. I was very happy to see the continuation of this joyous tradition when on a visit to the Cornell campus after forty years of my student days, I found the glee club giving an open air concert on the steps of the Willard Straight Hall.

Cornell University can boast of having practically the most scenic campus. The campus is fringed on two sides by a stream and a waterfall. On one side the waterfall is across a sizeable lake. The lake freezes in winter and provides canoeing in summer and skating in winter. I tried my hand boldly on both, but remained a novice. I could escape a disaster by coolly grabbing the emergency wire stretched across the width of the lake just before the water tumbled down the waterfall. The caretaker was quite pleased with the live test of the safety precaution taken by them when they stretched that wire. The campus was dotted with tennis courts. The desirous students could enroll as beginners. They also had a rifle club and students could learn to shoot with rifles. The main entertainment of the students and the studentesses is mutual entertainment by the institution of dating. The liberty in heterosexual meeting was extending slowly to the conservative sororities and fraternities existing all around the campus. Students were pointing to the progressive universities in the west where boys and girls were living in the same hostels. In general a tradition existed that limited sex among students to remain within bounds, but they were given full opportunity to choose their life partners when at school if possible. I sometimes wondered if the student unrest so visible in India could disappear if the custom of dating was introduced. Historically young love was an open door to the revolutionary activities in pre-revolution Russia. The communists always seriously used attraction between opposite sexes for revolutionary activity among youths. I found same sort of conditions in the J.L. Nehru University in Delhi where the campus and the co-education as well as the ascendancy of communist movement was conducive to dating as well as strikes. In U.S.A. an important pre-occupation of the students is to earn their living as students since the costs of education are high and not automatically met by the parents or the government. Every university has an office of student employment. This innovation of making it practical for students to partially earn for their studies could certainly invite more serious students to the university than just the more affluent people sending their wards to the schools. The education has to be based on broken or lengthened periods of stay in the schools than the current system. The vacations have to be free of educational stress so that a student can earn a handsome amount which can cover a good percentage of his expenses in the ensuing school session.

A liberal engagement of student employees in the administrative tail of the university will increase the efficiency as well as ease the agitations that pester the vicechancellors on account of the disgruntled administrative tail which is usually large in India. During my own employment as a demonstrator in Punjab university, I was so used to being handed a glass of water by a bearer when I was thirsty, that I was surprised to see our head of the department going to the corridor to the water fountain there to have a sip of water. Prof. Bhabha was one notable Indian scientist who visited the Physics department when I was at Cornell. He suggested that if I could work on the gamma ray spectra, I could later be useful in the nuclear energy programme in India. But I had already selected a project in Solid State Physics which I thought was more within the plans of using my services on return in the Punjab. I did not know at that time that the upheaval of partition will completely obscure development plans for the Punjab. About the time I left Cornell, A.R. Kidwai migrated from Michigan to complete his doctorate in Chemistry at Cornell. We became friendly and have remained so.

The Punjab Government which had selected me for training in the States had mentioned that they would like to have me establish a State standards laboratory for them and I had chosen my courses with that goal in view. Left to myself I might have elected theoretical physics which was very strong at Cornell in those days. Prof. Bethe and Prof. Feynman who was working on quantum electrodynamics which won him the Nobel Prize soon after, were very much sought after by graduate students. I was among the best pupils of Prof. Feynman as indicated by the results of his course tests. I had often discussed with him theoretical problems that were not clear in the textbooks. In line with my planning, after completing my work for the Ph.D. degree at Cornell, I shifted to the U.S. National Bureau of Standards at Washington D.C. for practical training arranged by the Indian Embassy. I worked with Prof. L. Marton in electron physics and in electron microscopy. Prof. Marton was a man of great energy and had a soft corner for trainees from India and other developing countries. When the tenure of my government stipend expired in early 1949, the Punjab riots had disrupted the conditions there and even the Punjab University staff and students were scattered in many towns of north India. I was, therefore, keen to look around for financial support to complete my work with Dr. Marton who very kindly asked me to contact the Director of Terrestrial Magnetism of the Carnegie Institution who sometimes engage graduate students for part time work. I was given such work for three months desired by me. I set up the wiring of the ionospheic chambers being rigged by them and after three months, he offered me a Carnegie fellowship for geophysics which altered my scientific career considerably.

The youth have many aspirations everywhere. On the campuses the first importance is to studies and second to heterosexual company. The weekends are usually devoted to extra-curricular activities like participation in hikes, dances, music, etc. Our students in India on the other hand are so obsessed by the imperative of examinations set by external examiners who could not be aware of the difficulties of the students and their teachers for studies in depth on account of the wide coverage of the syllabus in a superficial fashion. Thanks to the sports cult, recently when India found herself trailing woefully in the

Olympic meets, there is now considerable recognition and financial support to budding athletes. The problems that were faced by sports in universities are still faced by science in the universities. There is always great shortage of funds for support of individual scientists and institutions for scientific staff, equipment and books. The sports scene is much better now. We notice idolatry of cricketers and film stars. There has been great contribution from the organizers of adventure sports. Nehru was quite concerned with the spread of mountaineering in India perhaps because India was to protect a long mountainous frontier. The adventure sports have developed hiking and sailing to new heights. Some Indian adventurers have undertaken long sea voyages in tiny crafts, and have staked their grit on cross channel swimming. Wild life and marine parks have been created. Archeological adventurers have brought to the surface evidence of sunken cities off the coast of Gujarat. Cause of environment and preservation of habitat is served by combining these concerns with sports like bird watching and care of wildlife like the preservation of dwindling tigers, wild tropical forests, etc. Sports concern everyone. In school in India, hockey was my favourite game and I played for the neighbourhood and the college teams. Later I usually played regularly either volleyball or tennis. Tennis I learnt to play only at Cornell and later in departmental games I managed to get the trophy primarily by having a good partner for doubles matches. Now in later life when people go for golf or long walks, I have enough exercise in yoga and it is now a question of avoiding interruption in a regular routine. I must recommend to all to cultivate some pastime as this would be handy in old age when slowly the company dwindles to one's wife or a close friend or two. How many people are there who do not know what to do with themselves. They yearn for company when alone, but want to escape one if they are surrounded by company and are not prepared for it. They had not prepared by having a suitable pastime in which zero, one, two or three persons could join besides themselves. The British regard visiting a pub alone or with friends as a pastime. In India, people go to clubs mainly to have a drink or to play cards. The Cricket Club of India at Bombay could very well be called the cards club of India. Those who are better organized could have cultivated some lasting hobbies besides pastimes reading or writing make also excellent hobbies in addition to the usual arts or crafts. Mahatma Gandhi popularized spinning as a remunerative pastime for the masses. The folk in the village have much more commitment to arts and crafts like weaving and carving which are both devotional as well as earning skills. Watching television has been adopted by many old persons including my wife as a pastime and it certainly is entertaining as well as instructive. All the world over religious prayers and prescribed devotions had been adopted as a worthy activity for the old people. This way they would not get in the way of purposeful activity of the younger generation.

The period just after the war when I was at Cornell, was singularly free of violence. People had their fill of violence and had the guilt of Hiroshima on their mind. Even crime was at low key. We invariably left our rooms unlocked and any stuff left somewhere by mistake could be picked from there without any loss the next day. The young men and women were eloquent about social justice and even were prepared to accept nationalization and socialism to certain extent. But the Soviet rhetoric and Churchill's speeches ended the climate of peaceful coexistence. On the other hand majority of Americans are not averse to the use of violence. Now they have also perfected the art of pretending to be guarding human rights when violent, while only those who are opposed to their policy indulge in violently trampling on the human rights of others. There are more private guns than U.S. citizens in America. Now even children threaten their school teachers with violence. The games for children were around hunting of Red Indians and handling toy guns and armaments. But there is a silver lining: A new breed of children games is evolving based on the game theory and the computer where a child is led to the cooperative solution of games. Such invention of computer games for children would be good in India against communal and regional tensions arising randomly in India these days.

Ithaca gets pretty cold with about seven months of snowfall in the year. The scene is heavenly when the leaves turn colour in autumn. The craze for morning walks and jogging had not yet set in. I enjoyed my lonely morning walk in all kinds of weather and a swim when possible at the Bebee lake. From Ithaca, I visited few times New York city, Niagra Falls, Toronto, Ottawa, and Montreal in Canada and other university towns in Eastern United States.

One will do well to devote few minutes each day to think about his values, aims and means. Human mind has great potential and in order to allow it to achieve the same, introspection and meditation are excellent aids. Ever since the visit of Vivekananda to U.S.A. and subsequent acquaintance with professional *swamis* from India, the public associated some spiritual inclination with the Indians. I also could not stay away from experimenting with meditation and yoga. Weather permitting I would every day indulge in simple meditation and yoga by the side of the waterfall. In regular yoga learnt from an adept, one only learns to control the mind and dwell on the glimpse of ultimate reality behind the universe. In the process certain ability of clairvoyance, a believable glimpse of past lives and ability to discern future and occurrence hidden from view, etc., are developed. Any deliberate development and use of such abilities, it is said detracts from the goal of self-realization. I had no such ambition of becoming a Buddha, but I had scientific curiosity in the nature of such abilities. I believe I was surprised and overwhelmed by the success of my experiments. I could by mental concentration discover what might be happening elsewhere or what was to happen in the future a few times. But the mental effort was relentless and after my graduation from Cornell I never deliberately embarked on such errands. But, few times I could dream true about immediate future when sorely pressed about certain events and gained confidence from such dreams.

The Hindustan Association had sprung up in many universities and provided a platform for many Indian lecturers who were in U.S.A. or visited the country. We had a noted dancer from New York for Indian dances. Shri P. Kodanda Rao lectured on two occasions on Indian philosophy. In a series of lectures many local students and visitors gave talks on various aspects of Indian arts and literature. Around this time Z.A. Bhutto visited Cornell and found that there were too few Pakistani students to start a separate Pakistan Students Association. I explained to him that the Cornell Hindustan Association accepted students at Cornell besides Indians as members.

Noor-ul-Haque Khan, a Pakistani student from Lahore had travelled with me to Ithaca and we lived in the same rooming house at 118 Cook Street. We became close friends and many a time I depended on him during spells of bad cold that were unavoidable at Cornell. He once asked me blandly why I did not become a Muslim since he was certain that I would make a good Muslim. He was surprised that I was stuck with the nebulous beliefs of Hinduism. This set me explaining to him why Hinduism was proper for a modern man if he wanted some religion. He gave an interesting comment at the end of our discussions spread over a few days. He had spent twenty-five years of his life at Batala and Lahore among dozens of Hindus besides his Muslim friends and relations, and wondered why he never became acquainted with the fine points of Hinduism. Why Hindus failed in explaining their faith to the Muslims of India and Pakistan. I further clarified that I was certain there were innumerable Muslims who would make excellent Hindus. But Hindus believe that there is no point in flitting from one religion to another. For a fruitful life any spiritual path is equally valid. Pious and virtuous life does not exist in the mode of worship of one deity or another when all deities are only concepts and images of reality.

The youngest Indian under-graduate was Kanwar Lamba who had been granted a local embassy stipend by the Ambassador of India. He was later to become an important trade functionary in India. The oldest Indian student was Dr. Tulsa Ram, the poultry specialist come for acquiring a post-graduate degree in agriculture. He had come to U.S.A. leaving his wife and children back in India and was saving money and buying useful business and home gadgets for taking to India on completion of his course of studies. He once advised me to follow his example and save money for future life in India. This advice I disregarded stating that I believe in current life than in future life and I also invested when I travelled in the States or outside, towards my education and training. Another friend, Shri J.C. Kapur I had known from my school days. He later pushed the use of solar energy in India and has written books about contemporary India. Among the other students that I came in close contact were F. Dyson who came as post doctoral scholar with Prof. Bethe and later became a Nobel Laureate in Physics. I have also kept up my friendship with Dr. W.A. McAfee who had a brilliant career with the U.S. Army Signals and later was active in under-graduate physics education. Some of the American physics students also rose to eminent positions in biology or electronics.

There was constant emphasis on democratic norms on the campus. In India there was a tendency to convert democratic positions of responsibility into dictatorial offices. At the Cornell university every student organization had to accept a faculty adviser whose responsibility was to attend every meeting of the executive committee and to supervise the annual elections so that democratic procedures and the agreed constitutional provisions were scrupulously followed. The nominations to various offices were made through popularly appointed nominating committees or by a call for volunteers. No small caucus could highjack a campus organization. At no campus occurred strikes or protests by students or staff since the administrative procedures were spelled out in detail without any ambiguity and procrastination. The image of a police force is quite different in a free democratic country, than what I was familiar with in colonial India. For obtaining a Mexican visa, I had to attach a police report to my application. My immediate reaction was that since I did not know anyone in government or the police force, this may become difficult. Mr. Ker, the University Adviser for foreign students immediately reassured me that since I did not know anyone in the police force that was the proper reason for them to hand the police report across the table to me. I have only to approach the local police authority. Their not knowing me was sufficient recommendation. I obtained the police report as above. But I decided to save time and effort and to spend my brief vacation in Canada, where I visited, Montreal, Toronto, Thousand Islands and Ottawa. I was surprised to have preserved the memory as the best view of Toronto as observed from a road overbridge of the Catherine Street at night. At Montreal, I thought I might be able to use my French that I had laboriously learnt in India, but I did not succeed in the endeavour. The French Canadians assumed that I was speaking a non-European tongue when I did not speak English. I reached Ottawa during a Marian Congress with delegates from all over the world. There was an interesting encounter with a minor priest who wanted to bring me to the true religion. When I mentioned that I was a Hindu of the same faith as that of Mahatma Gandhi. He retorted that all those who do not accept the cross will go to hell after demise and Gandhi keeping me company there would be no consolation. I am sure that Catholics have advanced in religious tolerance much more now. The Pope himself has shown respect to Hindus and Hinduism. I have been to Canada couple of times later too. I went there to attend as a member of the Indian delegation to the triennial conference of the Commonwealth Defence Science Advisory

Committee. Most of the time was spent in Ottawa, but we visited Halifax as well as the frozen Tundra terrain. It was during this visit that our train got stuck in the wilderness because of the snow drifts both ahead and back that made the movement of the train impossible for more than thirty-six hours. My last visit was in 1987 for attending the International Union of Godesy and Geophysics General Assembly at Vancouver. My wife and I availed of an excursion visit to Victoria with an entertaining ferry ride and a visit to the Buchart gardens. I was struck with the thorough study of the Indian history and civilization at the University of British Columbia at Vancouver which also boasts of an excellent oriental museum.

I was never involved with excessive wardrobe. In India the accent was on simplicity and frugality so much so that even when I had sufficient funds, personal knick knacks and expensive clothing was my least priority. Thus when I had my first date with a girl friend whom I had met at Cornell during her short course in summer, everything that I had: my suit, shoes, watch, shirt or tie all looked shabby to me. My friends confirmed that being well dressed was important for an important first date and contributed liberally sundry dress items. Still I avoided borrowed plumage, only, I purchased a new watch on credit for the trip. I was duly impressed by the easy acquisition on credit of an expensive watch which lasted me for a long time. The visit to the central park in New York with my friend was a memorable one in another sense. I had dreamt of the central park with my girl friend few days earlier in explicit detail when I even did not know of the existence of that kind of place in a part of New York. I have visited the park again many times, but later the scene seemed rather prosaic. At that time the poetry within me was at its height, so much so that she had to tread on my toes to stop me from continuing with a dance when the music had already stopped.

Here I would mention a social get-together. A Canadian couple was quite popular in the department. They invited few friends from the graduate students and some faculty to their house for an anniversary party. It was a typical American party with mountains of sandwiches and an opulent bar with the husband acting as the bar tender and the wife entertaining the guests by party games and extempore dances. I protested that I did not drink, and they would not insist on my doing so, still they argued that if everyone went to hell, what would I do alone in heaven. They also challenged my spirit of scientific experimentation. I succumbed to the arguments and challenged the host to make a most mixed drink that he could. I realized later that I got drunk in that party. I harangued the pretty hostess about the great worth of Indian philosophy and gave her a discourse on the rise of civilizations. Having learnt that proper etiquette required an appreciative dance with host's wife if she would dance, I practically monopolized her for major part of the evening till she could extricate herself. I would gladly apologize to her for inflicting my dancing on her when I hardly knew how.

Mr. Mendenhall, the appointed guide for the moral life and in-charge of the university chapel was an enlightened Church of England priest. He had lost a son in some adventure in the northern regions of Canada. I had often interesting discussions with him regarding the religious beliefs of students in India and in U.S.A. Once he suggested that a talk should be arranged on the story of Rama and Sita. A south Indian student volunteered to do so. He illustrated his talk by reciting a number of couplets from *Ramayana*. These sounded like Sanskrit. Later I asked him if he was a scholar of Sanskrit to recite with such felicity, the *Ramayana* in the original. He corrected my impression, the quotations were from Kamban's Ramayana in Tamil with which he was entirely familiar.

The university was a fully integrated and discrimination free. I have mentioned earlier my black friend who was writing his Ph.D. thesis in theoretical Physics. I visited his family in New Jersey and later also in my subsequent visits to U.S.A. from India. He was living in a mixed locality not far from the Atlantic Ocean. Most of his neighbours were white. Every evening he would take me to the beach where often I would wade into the sea and enjoy my swim. His wife or children never accompanied us, and he himself did not touch the water. Once I asked him if he felt any racial discrimination in his locality. He said that there was none since he did not create any opportunity for his decent neighbours and the community to give expression to such prejudice. This reminded me of the statement of a prejudiced Hindu back home that he had never practised untouchability since the untouchables of his acquaintance kept their distance from him. However in the last fifty years, integration has come a long way from those times.

V

Washington D.C.

Americans have the same values as I had imbibed in India. They are open minded, sincere and ready to rectify if they admit to having made a mistake. In India democracy often amounts to the election of a temporary dictator. This is the reason we have the problem of "dissidence". In a democracy a majority means a preponderant number of representative human beings acting in concert on political and social issues. A statement that Hindus are in majority, so they must form the government is meaningless in a true democracy where every-one is first and foremost a human being. The people in USA are in general religious minded, but they do not wear their religion on their sleeve and would not interfere in any way with others in their own respective observance of religion. It was considered laudable if some one attended a church or synagogue but there was no pressure to conform. After two years at Ithaca, I moved to Washington D.C. where I was a guest worker at the U.S. Government National Bureau of Standards for about a year and then a Carnegie Fellow for research in Geophysics at the department of Terrestrial Magnetism of the Carnegie Institution of Washington for two years. Very early in my stay there I founded the Hindustan Club and many Indians working or studying at Washington joined it. Our centre of activities was the International Student House run by Quakers. The members were from among the local American professionals and foreigners working in foreign embassies or multinational organizations. The International Student house also had some residential accommodation for those who desired it and dining in facility requiring advance notice by one meal. They had spacious lounges, dining room, and a hall for celebrations and plays or lectures, etc. They had a resident director, an appointee of the Quaker headquarters at London. I am sure that there is a void in Washington when this centre had to close in the seventies due to paucity of funds.

The centre provided a clean club like atmosphere for students and others in Washington living rather at a distance from such facilities readily available on the campus of large universities. Every evening one could have some activity for participation like a game of volley-ball or table tennis, or meet friends at a tea or dinner, participate in party games or be involved in some ethnic or general entertainment event or listen to some topical discussion.

I took upon myself often to show some new arrival from India the city sights. My plan for sight seeing in Washington was rather simple. First one was taken to the top of the Washington Monument, so that the plan of the city and the famous landmark monuments could be identified. The tour then will include the visits to the Lincoln and the Jefferson memorials and a round of the Capitol building housing the American Houses of Representatives. If the time permitted and I was in the mood I took the guest to the Blue Ridge Mountain National Park or to the scenic drive along the creek to Chevy Chase. In my subsequent visits to Washington DC. I found some additional spots that have come up and are of tourist interest particularly the prestigious underground communication system and remarkable eating places across the river.

During my training attachment to the National Bureau of Standards, I had opted for electron microscopy and Dr. L. Marton was an authority on this subject. Besides carrying out some practical work on the electron microscopy of surface replicas, I was suggested the task of setting up a balance for the measurement of magnetic fields in electron lenses. The balancing of the field's pull on the Le Poole coil carrying a winding that reversed in the middle was done by the force of electrical induction from a surrounding coil. The arrangement was reproduced by a visiting student on his return to Brussells whom I visited during my return journey to India. I was rather pleased when I topped a test given by some visiting psychologists regarding intelligence to a large number of volunteers working on research projects in the Bureau. I also attended a short course on the administration for scientists and on this basis I published an article on this topic in Science and Culture on return to India. The verdict of many colleagues was that the article contained in a nutshell most of the material often filling large verbose books. In

1952, I could entertain Dr. Marton in my house at Delhi when at my suggestion to Prof. M.N. Saha, he was invited by the Science Congress Association to visit India. He also could see the electron microscope set up by one of his students at Calcutta. Towards the end of my tenure at the Bureau, at his recommendation the Indian embassy deputed me to attend a summer course on quantum electrodynamics and infrared detectors at the University of Michigan at Ann Arbor. Infrared detectors were becoming of considerable importance in defence applications. Another interesting visit was to a farm where I was a house guest and I could see various activities, on an American private farm of a reasonable size. I did not like the single rooms that could be rented for stay in a large city like Washington D.C. Only later when I had a better income as Carnegie Fellow, I could share an apartment with an officer in the India Supply Mission. My companion was expert in fast food cooking Bengali style and this saved us much time. I have noticed that going out to a restaurant is more time consuming than managing in own apartment with the availability of kitchen gadgets and large variety of tinned foods. The microwave heaters were not yet in vogue. With their advent home cooking has become still easier. I could also buy an old car. I was advised to go in for a good body and replace the engine by a re-built one. As a young researcher in the Carnegie Institution, I got 50 per cent concession on the price of a newly re-built engine. This was one of the ways in which private industry showed their appreciation and encouraged scientific research. In India such concessions are yet a dream, being available only to key men who might be inclined to give favours in return. Most people own cars which are left parked in the streets at night. Once the streets close to my apartment were so full that I had to hunt for a parking place few blocks away. I felt so awkward next morning when I could not remember where my car was parked and took about half an hour roaming the streets before locating the same. The Americans have to work fairly hard both for making money as well as for support of the household since even minor repairs/ alterations by professionals cost a tremendous amount. They have, therefore, little idle time and the play and entertainment have to be planned in advance. It is not feasible to drop in unannounced at any one's residence and expect to find him ready to while away some time with the visitor. This sort of random encounter is regarded as a test of close friendship or relationship in underdeveloped countries. Still the

Americans make very good friends and I have seen my American friends readily sparing their time and resources to converse with a friend, or to be of assistance. A friend who was a doctor would gladly prescribe for me directly to the pharmacist and charge no fees. Once the brakes of my car failed and a friend of mine came to my rescue by guiding me at practically 5 miles an hour in his car to a repairman about 10 miles away.

With Washington as base I travelled to mid-western as well as southern states. As part of field experience I used to accompany a geologist of the institution to pick up samples from road cuts for paleo-magnetic studies from all over the eastern mountainous region. In other trips we went to the coal mining region of West Virginia and Kentucky and the hilly terrain of upper New York state. The countryside in the coal belt was a disappointment. It was so poor and we rarely came across a worthwhile place for refreshments, etc. Whenever the department learnt of the plan anywhere of a large explosion, they would plan to occupy some sites for obtaining seismic records of the explosion. The explosions were made either for construction purposes or for Defence testing and the seismic records were obtained to understand the deep crustal structure of the earth, as well as to learn in general the travel of seismic wave signals in the upper crust. Once I had set up the seismic measuring equipment near some farmer's property, when the owner learnt that I was there to measure the earth's shaking caused by the expected explosion about 50 kms away, he thought it fit to sue the institution for damages to his property by earthquake waves that we were causing and measuring there! My colleagues and I enjoyed these jaunts and travels. I called scientists like us engaged in geophysical exploration "cowboys in science". One of our colleagues Prabhat Kumar Bhattacharya was a great sport. He sang and danced beautifully. Later from his teaching job in India, he spent a year on invitation in Russia where he won great honour from the Russian youth organization for his fine presentation of Indian and American music and dance. Alas, he died quite young from burns while trying to save his wife from burning in a kitchen accident. The wife survived him by few hours.

I was sharing my apartment with a Bengali friend who was working in some diplomatic post. He was very much married, but his wife was in India. He became very fond of an American girl and he managed to have a passport showing him as unmarried so that at a pinch he could convince the girl about his single worth. The girl was disillusioned only after about one year when he was transferred back to India. I was pretty certain that I would be returning to India on the completion of my studies and had sincerely warned everybody especially any American girls who might become over friendly. I humorously termed marrying and bringing an American girl to a middle class home in India as "cruelty to animals". Couple of Indian students known to me who had brought American wives to India either returned with them to the States or had themselves divorced. Up to the end of World War II, the old value of fidelity and lifelong love prevailed. Later the people became more mobile and agile and the old value shed its lustre. Single persons became keen on experimentation and keen for mutual freedom. Smoking, promiscuity and drugs followed in succession. During the fifties almost every young male or female smoked. Only after the rise and fall of the hippie cult and from dangers inherent in sexual and drug abuse, value of abstinence has again emerged on the American scene and in the nineties smoking is almost totally gone. On the other hand in India the screen heroes and villains all smoke and smoking and drinking has been catching on as part of good management and commercial relations. In 1973, when I was transferred on promotion to become a director of an Armament Institute in India, the then scientific adviser particularly advised me that even if I did not drink normally, still I should allow myself and others social drinking when I will have many senior officers of the armed forces joining me socially, etc. I was certain that the advice was out of step with the Indian ethos. I continued to avoid drinking and I hope I encouraged among the army officers and personnel, the fashion of abstinence. An Indian friend who later joined UNESCO purchased a new car. He agreed to take me and another friend on cost sharing basis to a tour of the southern states. In those days colour bar north of Washington D.C. was almost non-existent but it existed in traces in the south but rarely extended to foreigners. Few days earlier we had come across an article in the newspapers by an angry black citizen. He expressed surprise at the refusal of service to him at certain bars in the south when he was promptly welcomed if he went there sporting an East Indian style turban. We toured all over the southern states right up to New Orleans and returned unscathed by any colour bar excepting at one place where one entered a bar and then could pass on to a restaurant for sit-in dinner. From the number of vehicles parked outside we guessed the food to be good, so we entered the place and tried to make a beeline for the restaurant ignoring the bar. We were jolted by the sudden hush in the crowded bar and then a brazen waiter addressed the person in the lead to the effect that did not we know that the service counter for coloured people was on the side of the main building. I told him that we were visitors from India and usually we had not faced such a choice in the many restaurants we had already patronized. On this the proprietor came forward full of apology stating that they did not practice any colour bar and we were welcome to get service anywhere in the restaurant or the bar. Only they could not hold back their surprise since non-whites had never claimed service in that restaurant. I reassured them that though such discrimination was unfair, we were not strangers to it in the reverse direction in our own country few decades ago. In our house if a white person entered by chance without the lady of the house being prepared for it, she would have to purify herself by a bath and the house by a thorough washing of the floor after the white person had left!

Another experience concerned driving on the highway. It was late in the evening and we were trying to reach suitable lodging for the night. The road was almost clear of traffic being the time of the evening meal. I was driving rather fast, and hugging the centre line. An approaching car was also doing the same and it became an accidental game of chicken. We all became alert only when the two cars grinded past each other, perhaps brushing flat the outer millimetre of each car. The two cars stopped for a moment to assess the damage. The distance between the two stopped cars was not less than a kilometre, and then both continued their respective travel. I have since then been warning everyone never to closely hug the centre line but remain few inches at least away to own side of the pavement.

It was in Washington that I got friendly with a Pakistani student from East Bengal who later rose to be the leader of Bangladesh when it became independent. He was very sincere in his desire that India and Pakistan should get over their differences about Kashmir and we jointly prepared a paper for possible Indo-Pakistani accord. Basically it visualized election of negotiators separately from Pakistan's northern territories which had been detached from the original J&K State as well as Pak occupied or Azad Kashmir, Ladakh, Kashmir valley, and fourthly Jammu. These negotiators will first decide if they want continuation of the J&K State and declare their intention of remaining with Pakistan or with India if the entire State has to be partitioned. We brought the scheme to the attention of authorities in the two embassies and the US State Department. The Indian and Pakistani official position remained that they had a right to the entire State. In 1950, I prepared a paper on "World Technical Mission" and sent it to the UN authorities. I received a reply that they were already developing an International Development Programme and will certainly consider the issues concerning resources and the development philosophy mentioned in my paper. One day I was asked by the information official of the Indian Embassy, if I could be nominated for a public discussion on the Korean problem along with the spokesmen from the British Embassy, and some columnists from the media. They did not wish to send an official spokesman from the Embassy of India. I believe I did appropriate justice to the task, no-one during the discussion or later found fault with the Indian views as presented by me. I happened to be quite prepared for such a task as only few days earlier after a friendly discussion in the department's luncheon meeting, I had been asked to give in writing my appreciation of the Korean problem as well as the Soviet-Indian relations which looked biased to the director.

Dr. M.A. Tuve, the Director of the Department of Terrestrial Magnetism was a very much respected man of science. Once we discussed if the scientists should spend their whole working life in the pursuit of science or seek to rise in the administrative ladder by becoming presidents of universities, etc. Dr. Tuve rubbed off his keen desire on me that a scientist should avoid non-scientific jobs. He refused outside offers. I could easily get a job later when in India in the F.A.O. or get into the Indian management pool when it was first mooted in 1954, but I chose not to apply. I vividly recall the day when my fellowship was extended by one year. Just couple of days earlier I had attempted to explain how India was friendly with Russia when Dr. Tuve held the Russian dictatorship as fully exposed to be anti-people. My recipe for communism was friendship and demonstration of development through democracy. India was attempting this through cooperative living of its people. India's ideal was universal peace and goodwill. Dr. Tuve was a great dreamer about world peace and the leadership of the USA. I remember his asking me to report to him in his office next day, and if I wished to add or alter anything in my paper on India and the Soviet Union which I had given to him. In 1951, there were the McCarthy days in Washington and I expected to hear goodbye as my fellowship was expiring in a few days. Suddenly in his office Dr. Tuve fished out couple of apples and threw one for me to catch. While both of us were munching apples, he broke the news that the institution had thought it fit to extend my fellowship by one year.

I became a regular frequenter of the Washington Quaker meeting. The Director of the National Bureau of Standards was also a Quaker. The democratic priest-less Quaker brotherhood of friends is entirely ethics based and exemplary for world culture. The chief volunteer of the meeting is known as the clerk of the meeting. His duties include calling of the meeting and issuing information of the meeting. He introduces any invitee or any important person who happens to be attending and often introduces a theme for added meditation. The quakers do not aim to capture any social positions. They sit in the meeting in silence, until someone decides to make short utterance known as message from the silence of God. After some silent meditation interrupted by a few such messages, the meeting comes to a close when one shakes hand with the next neighbour. I wish I had kept record of the fine messages I got from others in these meetings. One message tried to clear up the Biblical miracles by saying that in those days perhaps angels visited the world from their different universe, but they do not do so now. The quakers believe in the inner light and in non-violence. They have been the bulk of conscientious objectors to army draft. They are, however, Christians in faith and hope for salvation through their faith in the Cross of Christ. They, however, believe Christ to be living in their hearts.

I had met earlier a Dutch resistance member at Cornell and few times we shared the same platform about our respective war time surroundings. At Washington I made friends with one Richard Tietz who was living in the international student house and had been an active anti-Nazi in war time Germany. During my return journey to India I travelled to Frankfurt from London in order to meet his parents and brother there. They were rather impressed by my German which I had retained from my earlier studies in India. We could happily converse in German about the life in Washington, and post-war Germany and in India during the war.

The Hindustan Club had a routine gathering once a month at the international centre involving impromptu or sometimes rehearsed programmes after dinner which was optional for those who had sent advance intimation. A student from East Pakistan was a keen classical dancer. He gave few times dance items around the stylized identities of the Hindu gods and human incarnations of God. We humoured him when he claimed the dances to belong to Pakistani culture. Little did he know at that time that East Pakistan would later seek freedom from Pakistan on the grounds of distinct culture.

Towards the end of my stay in Washington, some colleagues with whom I joined, decided on a holiday trip to Florida and stay at some beach resort in Miami. My colleagues were very considerate and made detours on the way so that I could meet some friends whose addresses I had collected. A girl friend who had some allergy in the environment at Washington had moved to some family property at Miami. She undertook to put up the whole car load at her house in Miami. The Disney World did not exist in Florida at that time. Still she managed to show us all major spots of tourist interest and we had plenty of time on the Florida beaches. I had occasion however to visit both the Disney Land near Los Angeles and the Disney World in Florida. Either one is a complete resort catering to all kinds of people, young and old.

Washington's Birthday was celebrated in a particularly interesting way by the commercial establishments of the town. Most stores offered discounts on part of their merchandise on that day on first come first served basis. They also showed in the shop window the discounted prices of certain items including some costly items given away free. In front of many stores there were overnight queues and certain groups took turns one by one in the queue. The shopping on that day was very popular with students. I once picked up a used standard office typewriter at 10 per cent of its price and it is still in use after more than forty years with a nephew of mine in India. Few months earlier my own portable typewriter and a movie camera were stolen from my apartment when I had left the key on the peg for some purpose with the lift-man. The camera was replaced at half price by the manufacturer on my application. Research scholars often got such concession from the manufacturers. The crime of theft is not common.

The police thought it must have been a teenager visiting someone in the large apartment house. The criminal violence that has increased later in American cities is rather disturbing. Perhaps children do need more supervision and curtailment of too much liberty so that the values imbibed by future generations remain stable and constructive.

Washington's theatre in the round was my favourite for occasional evening entertainment. It was a small theatre and played usually famous American and European plays. There was no barrier between the stage and the audience which sat on terraced chairs around the stage on the floor. The first serious lesson in contract bridge, I had was from Dr. Fred Singer who needed a partner, while I had only just graduated from auction bridge to contract one. Dr. Singer became a famous Geophysicist and was instrumental in myself being invited to an International Conference on Unity of Sciences in Washington D.C. in 1984.

Dr. Frank Press of Lamont Observatory had begun frequency analysis of seismic signals. He visited the D.T.M. to talk to us about his work. I also visited Lamont. It is a pity that Dr. Maurice Ewing, the energetic director of Lamont had an untimely death when engaged on the Mohole project in mid-Atlantic. An Indian research assistant of his was recommended for a senior job in India when I was the scientific adviser to the Navy, but he did quite well staying put at Lamont. Couple of times he was invited for lectures to India. Dr. Nagata who had explained from chemical consideration certain magnetic reversals in paleomagnetic rock samples, visited us. A scientist from South Africa brought some seismograms from rock-bursts there. I could, using my method of analysis of the reverberation tails in seismograms, derive values of the depth of the Moho there which agreed with his values laboriously seen from the analysis of full travel time curves.

Many world figures in science visited the DTM at Washington D.C. Dr. S.D. Chatterjee of Calcutta came on invitation and helped the institution improve their Geiger counters. We became friends since then. Unfortunately he is now wholly bed-ridden. I came to know Dr. Gutenberg, Dr. Richter, Prof. Maurice Ewing, and Dr. Frank Press there. Dr. Gutenberg wanted a more comprehensive theory of the origin of storm microseismic on which I was carrying out some work. He and later Prof. Darbyshire became partial to the theory published by me after my return to India after some further work. Dr. Tuve thought very highly of my work on the scattering of seismic waves and my correct emphasis on the conversion of P waves to S waves back and forth during scattering. Dr. Roger Revelle when in station worked in particle physics at Derwood.

Dr. Tatel was the right hand man of Dr. Tuve for deep crustal seismology and the geophysical orientation to entire research programme. The institution possessed a cyclotron for research in particle physics and reactions of radiation on genes. Famous cosmic ray physicist Dr. Bush and statistician Dr. Vestine were engaged at the peak of their findings. Dr. Tuve's policy was that each scientist was free to pursue his researches without the straitjacket of set goals by the institute except that all efforts should be made at the extreme forward edge of any discipline. They were thus always working on some new and challenging areas. Besides choosing the subject of microseisms which was controversial, I had picked up the subject of scattering of seismic waves and also insisted on the interpretation of seismograms under the conditions of gradual increase of speeds with depth, thereby reducing the calculated depth of the Moho. Incidentally I could also make a thorough study of the recently received U.S. Government publications on the physics of under-water sound. This became useful to me for naval research when I was back in India. My theory about the origin of microseisms published in 1960 received favourable comments from the Chairman of the International Commission on Microseisms in 1983 when I was also elected a member of this commission.

To continue with the happenings at Washington, Dr. Tuve offered to recommend me to the U.S. Government if I desired to continue to work in the States, but in earlier discussions with him I had held forth that I should take my expertise to India who had spent hard-to-get foreign exchange on my deputation to the States. The Embassy was, therefore, alerted to arrange my passage to India which was now to be in two stages, Washington to London and then after some wait till sea passage could be booked from London to Bombay. The Education Ministry had advised that very likely I would be offered a lectureship in the Punjab University Physics Department housed in the government college at Hoshiarpur, Punjab. Dr. Tuve had in the meanwhile also suggested my name to Prof. M.N. Saha for possible work in Geophysics for which he found me most suitable. I made good-bye visits to Harvard, Columbia, and Cornell universities to meet some friends and then sailed from New York to London in the first week of July 1951.

VI

India Again and Naval Research

I travelled from New York to London by the merchant vessel Queen Mary. On reaching London I was told to be prepared to travel after one month to Bombay by boat. The High Commission had reserved my accommodation in some hostel and granted a liberal daily allowance for stay while awaiting forward passage. I used the interval for sightseeing in England and Europe and also to attend the IUGG General Assembly at Brussells to which I had contributed a paper from DTM. I discovered that though the organizers expected me to read my paper in the meeting of the International Association of Seismology, in those days one could attend the General Assembly only as a member of a national delegation and the national delegation from India had already been nominated and had arrived. The head of the delegation was a meteorologist who could not on his own take me in his delegation. He must first get clearance from Delhi, which he eventually got on the day of the inauguration. During the elections at the end of the assembly, I was elected as a member of the executive committee of the International Association. On reaching Delhi, I was asked to report to Government College, Hoshiarpur, Punjab and join the Punjab University department of Physics which was housed there. The Punjab Government officials at Simla also disclosed that the Defence Science Organization had requested my services to be transferred to them and since this might be a better job to suit my training abroad, I could await at Delhi their offer since the Ministry of Education had already agreed to transfer my services to the Central Government. Though everyone seemed to have agreed, still the bureaucratic delays and clearance from the Union Public Service

Commission took two months for me to join the Defence Science Organization. Everything had to be meticulously done in long hand in files after sending and receiving letters. No one trusted his ears of messages by phone. The bureaucrat looked all the time over the shoulder that he may not be caught making a mistake. Prof. D.S. Kothari was the head of the organization in honorary capacity, continuing his professorship at Delhi University. He had a difficult job regarding the administration of his charge. He was used to University affairs, often subject to individual pulls, while in the Central Government the bureaucratic rule prevailed as well as overt and covert antagonism of the middle rungs of the armed forces who felt the civilian run science organization an attempt by the upstart Government of India to encroach on the domain of the armed forces. My immediate job was to join as under-study to Dr. G.E. Gale, an admiralty scientist on loan to the Indian Navy as their Scientific Adviser. A number of senior officers in the Navy including the Chief of Naval Staff were British officers and they were somewhat more cooperative with Dr. G.E. Gale knowing the good work, the scientists in U.K. did for the Navy.

I am indebted to Dr. G.E. Gale for much advice and encouragement. Dr. Gale had already submitted plans for setting up two naval laboratories, one for physical and oceanographic research at Cochin and another for chemical and metallurgical research in the Naval dockyard at Bombay. He asked me to learn afresh the physics of underwater sound and Oceanography and to draw on the basis of titles discussed with him, project appreciations for the Cochin laboratory. Navy naturally had interest in many areas of science and technology besides what could be planned for next couple of years for the two proposed naval laboratories. These interests were to be pursued by our office at Naval Headquarters. We had some work being done at the Psychological Research Wing of the Defence Science Organization, and the Institute of Physiology and Allied Sciences working in a nucleus form at the Defence Science Laboratory presided over by Dr. Kothari. We also liaised with the meteorological department in their accumulation of weather, waves and tides data. I had to travel to various Naval establishments all along the coast of India for assessing the possible use to naval research of the technical and production facilities there. As soon as the nucleus of the physical laboratory was set up at Cochin, I spent one year from March 1953 as its first officer-in-charge. In 1954, Dr. G.E. Gale returned to the Admiralty in London and I was selected to succeed him and I moved with my wife from Cochin to Delhi (I had got married in 1952 while serving at Delhi).

While at Cochin itself, I had started some work on Oceanography and on microseisms which I progressed now by occasional visits there and encouraging young scientists whom we had recruited there. The seismographs, recording equipment, books on underwater sound were brought by me from the D.T.M. We soon had a full range of instruments for physical Oceanography and the authority to dove-tail our oceanography work with various naval vessels not only for our own projects but also of coastal Universities like Kerala and Andhra Universities. We had a wave recorder operating at Trivandrum, a microseismic station at Cochin, anomalous radar range observations at Jamnagar. Bathythermographs were operated from many naval vessels and the laboratory developed calibration equipment for these. In 1954 there was a Commonwealth Conference on Oceanography under the auspices of the N.I.O. in England. I was sent as the sole Indian delegate to attend it. The conference highlighted the problem of measurement of biological production in the oceans. (Ultimately in 1978, I gave an easy method of assessing the biological content from the fluctuation of echo intensities from sea bottom). My method is still awaiting use in the exploration of fisheries. In the conference and the meetings with the NIO scientists and their exhibits I got acquainted with Dr. G.E.R. Deacon and other British Oceanographers notably Dr. Longuet-Higgins and Dr. J. Darbyshire who both had made important contributions in the area of microseisms. On my return to Delhi I was elected the secretary of the National Committee of Oceanography set up by the Central Board of Geophysics of which I had become a member earlier. There were plans to set up a National Institute of Oceanography in India which was later set up at Goa. For the time being an Oceanography Research Unit was set up at Cochin at first in the naval laboratory and later in separate quarters at Ernakulam across the bay from the naval laboratory.

Around this time Prof. E.C. LaFond, an oceanographer of the US Electronics Laboratory at La Jolla joined the Andhra University at Waltair close to Visakhapatnam as an expert in Oceanography. We developed good rapport and naval ships afforded working space for the Andhra University scientists.

The scientists at the Cochin laboratory made important contribution in Oceanography and underwater sound from the very inception of the laboratory. We carried out seismic travel experiments in the ocean off Cochin, and measured the opacity of near shore waters. I conclusively showed the acoustic scattering in the ocean to be primarily from bio-plankton. We were the first in the world to meaningfully use radar for the study of sea roughness. The method was independently established later in the Soviet Union as a research tool.

During my stay at Cochin I enjoyed the rich cultural events there: Onam (new year) festival, Kathakali dances, prayers at temples by bursting crackers, single dancer's rendering from the epics, etc. I was the house guest of one of the organisers of the famous festival in which the gods and goddesses are taken in a procession of elephants and the attendants perform with drums and whisks. The Kerala boat race passed near our house close to the naval jetty. There were a number of picnics at neighbouring beaches. I always enjoyed research work on board ocean going vessels and had never any complaint of sea sickness. From Delhi I sometimes had an occasion to participate in Naval exercises involving visits to Sri Lanka, Laccadive islands or the Minicoy Island.

During the International Geophysical Year, I was invited to participate in the South Pacific Expedition of the Scripps Institute of Oceanography, La Jolla, California. I joined the expedition at Lima in Peru after flying from Bombay to Lima *via* New York. I measured the fluctuation of the echoes from sea bottom in connection with my proposal for the estimation of biological content at any place. Where the experimental catches showed almost biological desert condition, I could also predict the same from my acoustic echo experiment. The expedition took core samples and measured thermal conditions along the route from Lima to Easter Island and then to La Jolla. I stayed at La Jolla as house guest of Prof. R.W. Raitt who was one of the leaders of the expedition. The Raitts had a most beautiful house and they were perfect hosts. I travelled from San Francisco to Bangkok by a Military Air Transport Service aircraft of the U.S. Army and then by an Air India flight on to Calcutta. The MATS flight was quite an experience. There were overnight stops at Hawaii and Manila. A packed lunch was supplied to each passenger before the beginning of the flight. The flight coupon served as an identity card for use of military base facilities at way-side stops including shopping at military canteen stores. During my two weeks stay with Raitts, I visited the California Institute of Technology and the Disney Land. The visit to Cal. Tech. was also memorable as I could meet once again Prof. R.P. Feynman N.L. there.

The Easter Island is an isolated outpost of civilization and has its own secrets regarding the migration of its inhabitants presumably by raft from South America. There is the mystery of the large statues of an unidentified leader lying around the island. The administration is entrusted to Chilean Navy and the population looks forward to one or two tourist ships touching the island to secure some peculiar carved figures from the islanders, I was made to jump the plank as one crossing the equator on the vessel for the first time. I was rudely awakened once when a flying fish landed on my bunk through the porthole. Many shipmates suffered from dysentery, but luckily I escaped. During one of my night watches, I was thrilled to see the sharp rise in the profile of the sea bottom as displayed by the echo-sounder when the ship crossed a hidden sea mount. Next morning Dr. Fisher pinpointed it on his charts.

There was considerable worldwide activity towards studies to be carried out in the Indian Ocean in the extended IGY programme. About twenty-two ships from various countries took part at various times. I held a long discussion with the Defence Minister who had earlier been approached by the coordinator of the international programme regarding the desirability of India's full participation. This was during a flight with him from Delhi to Cochin. He showed his agreement to provide a Naval frigate for oceanographic studies for three months. The programme of the expedition was finalized at an inter-governmental conference in Copenhagen in 1961 which I attended as an adviser to the Indian delegation headed by Dr. D.N. Wadia. The delegation also visited the oceanographic laboratories of Denmark. For the first time, I experienced the uncanny sunshine late at night at Copenhagen.

A highlight of my official advice to the Navy was to ignore the opinion of some key officers that the building of war vessels was not feasible for India. I was of the firm opinion that immediate steps should be taken for building some relatively simpler war vessels so that in about ten years we could embark on serious ship-building for the Navy. I am certain that eventually India will be looked to for assuring peace and prosperity in the countries trading across the Indian Ocean. India has also to strengthen its deep sea fishing fleet.

Especially with the personality of Krishna Menon, the Defence Minister and his known equation with Jawaharlal Nehru, the Prime Minister, the armed forces were very jealous of their domain sliding into the clutches of the civilian nominees of the Central Government. In patriotic duties and assessments the Government and the forces were of the same mind, but there was gulf of difference in the claimed and aimed privileges for the uniformed personnel and the Gandhian accent on simple living to which government paid lip service. The scientific adviser and his defence science organization were kept at an arm's length from the working and the problems of the services. The scientific adviser had to get official missives from the Minister about his right to be consulted. The Defence Secretary or the Defence Minister did take the uniformed officers to task when they made obvious mistakes in their mistaken confidence about technical matters in themselves. They had constructed a whole lot of hangers and grounded many heavy equipments on an island and reclaimed land without determining the soil properties. The foundations started settling down causing considerable damage to the buildings and the installed equipment. Similar planning was made for newly reclaimed land around Cochin island. Krishna Menon on his first inspection visit asked the Naval construction engineers in uniform if they had consulted the scientists provided to the service whether the soil will be able to bear the planned load. The answer was no. I was actually present during this exchange. One could see that the civilian scientists were not thwarted from themselves taking the initiative and seeking technical problems and giving solutions before the Naval Commanders became aware of the actual formulation of the problem and its possible solution. They had become so accustomed to readymade instructions regarding equipment or tactics from the fallout from admiralty documents that were unclassified and freely available. Even smallest unimportant details would be referred to them for clarification. At Naval

Headquarters, however, there was slightly better atmosphere because of the past acceptance of Dr. G.E. Gale as a scientist in touch directly with the admiralty. I continued to attend the weekly meeting of the Deputy Chief of Naval Staff from which I could sometimes sense an issue requiring my scientific initiative. Thus began the early moves regarding the construction of war vessels, and the setting up of a Naval Specifications holding organization. The Chief of Naval Staff suggested increase in work efficiency through job analysis and work study. In the Defence Science Laboratory we organized a course on work study which led eventually to the establishment of the Institute of work study at Mussoorie. In order to carry out some operational research studies and for better liaison with the Defence Science Organization I spent my afternoons after full summer day's work at Naval Headquarters, at the defence science laboratories housed in the building of the National Physical Laboratory. I had an office along with couple of scientists there too. Prof. Kothari often was present in the scientific seminars and evening discussions where scientists presented their project plans or results. The accent was on operational research, i.e., the most effective use of existing weapons.

Krishna Menon was most energetic in promoting better performance of the Indian defence industries. He wanted them to utilize their full capacity and to go for industrial production for national use when there might be a lull in defence production orders. He also felt that the prosaic technical development organization of the army must be handed over to the Scientific Adviser as the Director General of a new Defence Research and Development Organization. This was done. A large number of uniformed officers came into the organization hugging also their promotion channels in the parent service. Many steps have since been taken to improve the situation. A large technical development establishment mainly concerned with specifications for defence purchases became a Defence Research Laboratory (Materials) under the new dispensation at Kanpur. Little did I imagine that I was to spend a large part of my career in defence research as head of this laboratory. Because of my experience in the U.S. National Bureau of Standards and membership of the prestigious American Society of Testing Materials as well as qualification from Cornell in Engineering Materials, the choice narrowed on me for steering this largest laboratory in India at that time into creative and significant materials research.

The most economical use of scientists by the defence in a developing country was in operational research for the evaluation of weapons allied with the state of training of the troops in the specific environment. There was speedier progress in the Navy for acceptance of scientists in their war games and Naval exercises. I was at hand during the periodic exercises of various groups of fleet. Sometimes the exercises were held jointly with ships of other friendly countries. The British submarines sometimes assisted in live training of the Indian vessels for underwater detection and evasion exercises. Later India had own submarines purchased or loaned from abroad. A Commonwealth Defence Science Advisory Committee was quite active in those days before we began to be more dependent on Soviet equipment. I attended their triennial conferences in Delhi in 1953 and Canada in 1956. The highlight of this conference was the introduction to defence problems in very cold and severe conditions of the Tundra. We were becoming aware of such problems in the defence of our Himalayan borders. During return from Canada I had an opportunity to visit some laboratories in U.K. particularly their newly started researches on the use of semi-conductors for infrared detection, etc.

It was decided that the army officers should be educated in the significance of nuclear energy and the effects of atomic bombs. I was asked by the Scientific Adviser to plan few lectures and deliver them at the Infantry School, Mhow. The three lectures I delivered covered the basic principles, the putting together of an Atomic Bomb and the effects of a nuclear explosion as well as need of proper shelters especially for command posts. I clarified that the real protection was to avoid a nuclear war by deterrent preparation or through diplomacy. The lectures were evidently convincing and I was asked to deliver them again at the Jabalpur establishment. The commandant of the school at Mhow gave me transport and a young student officer as escort for visits to Mandu and Indore nearby. It was thus that I could visit the famous ruins of the ancient capital city of Mandu. These ruins also commemorate the love story of the last ruler Baaz Bahadur and Roop Mati, a courtesan who was loyal unto death. These ruins are still studied by architects for their originality and grandeur. Mhow is also close to Indore, the ancient seat of some Hindu dynasties and Indore has imposing temples, picture galleries and libraries.

The Defence Science Laboratory had grown into a conglomerate of many disciplines and there was a move to branch off so that distinct disciplines have better opportunity to grow. The branching off was eventually carried out and the nucleus staff went from it to form new establishment, e.g., for technical training in work study, for researches in guided missiles, gun and ammunition design, for development of explosives and tanks, etc. The naval aspect of such researches was duly projected by me.

Earlier I had been the convener of a metallurgical conference in which the blueprint for a national metallurgical laboratory as well as for defence metallurgy project was finalized. Jawaharlal Nehru took personal interest in these plans. Dr. Kothari was himself guiding research in explosive fracture of metals, shaped charges and the reduction of factory generated pollution. About a dozen laboratories were started at different places by pioneers coming from the Defence Science Laboratory. Some scientists undertook a mathematical analysis of naval tactics. Selection of personnel by job analysis and psychological test batteries were first applied for naval work. The youngman who began research on naval tactics later became an authority on coding and the one who assisted me in seismic experiments at Cochin became an expert on antenna and electronic warfare and soon came to head a defence electronics laboratory.

A job in Delhi was considered highly profitable for organization contacts, but for pushing oneself, a different kind of personality is required. I was too much conscious of own ability to use any crutches of favour to find stepping stones. I was in the Navy list of principal staff officers and as such I had access to major civic or military functions in Delhi. The Chief of Naval Staffs annual dinner was always a memorable occasion.

During the selection of the first batch of students for the proposed National Defence College, a post extra to the cadre was created so that I could be nominated to fill the seat allotted to the Defence R & D Organization. During the course, I was given special leave by the Ministry to attend the Inter-governmental Oceanography Conference at Copenhagen referred to earlier. I had already served NHQ for about six years and when offered the directorship of the Kanpur Laboratory at the end of the course I welcomed the change particularly since that would be an inter-disciplinary and inter-service challenging job.

A national defence college course is a comprehensive opportunity to understand the national interest and the steps, philosophical and practical that would promote the security, prosperity and international regard for India. The course is divided into various studies ending with national security. There is competitive preparation of papers which are thoroughly discussed and then a consensus issued as a paper to authorities for information and action. There were lectures by well known authorities and personalities. Among the lecturers that graced the college rostrum were Jawaharlal Nehru, Maharajkumar of Sikkim, Tarlok Singh, etc. My course mates included many senior officers: General Arora, Admiral Kohli, General Batra, General Sartaj Singh, etc. The students travelled all over India both for grasping the size and terrain of its borders as well as cultural and industrial complexes in the country. Thus I could travel extensively along the borders of the Jammu and Kashmir State, to certain border outposts with Tibet, Rajasthan and Gujarat borders, Kohima, Bom De La, and also the industrial complexes in the east as well as in the south. We were taken to attend Air, Army, and Navy exercises as well as displays of modern equipments. I had always been inclined to the study of history as a hobby. The library of the college helped me to indulge in this. I was the youngest officer in the course and gladly undertook making comprehensive summaries of relevant books for my team mates.

The stay in the college helped me in writing later my book *Science and Technology in India's Transformation* published in 1986 by the Concept Delhi. This book was released by the President of India from the Rashtrapati Bhawan.

VII

Marriage and Family

There is a well known novel *Jean Christophe* by Romain Rolland, where the hero flits from one love to the next; every time it seems like true love, but is doomed to burst after a while. To the tradition bound whether in India or in Europe, this occurrence was considered progressive in the sense that young men and woman were on the look out themselves for a proper mate. There are however inherent difficulties in this mode of the progressives. In USA, on the University campus there was full freedom for mixed friendship, still so many of my friends moved from one girl friend to the next. Up to the end of the second world war, the old values of loyalty and fidelity confined a person to a single heart throb before marriage and to his spouse after his or her marriage. But about this time people became more mobile physically as well as mentally. Children should be left alone to learn themselves and campus promiscuity resulted. Almost everyone started smoking. Only much later, after the rise and fall of the hippie cult and common knowledge of sexually transmitted diseases including AIDS has a reaction set in. Now smoking has evaporated from the scene in America, though it is very much in view in India due to the time lag for fashions to reach there from the west.

The traditional view of heterosexual love is that of husband-wife relationship, i.e., for keeps, not only for this life but for ever after. Behind the arranged Indian marriage, there is the ideological underpinning of fidelity in wedlock. In the modern experimental situation, any excessive ardour only repels the beloved. Any affair to last depends on mutual skill in demonstration of attraction as well as a tinge of indifference. Pre-marital sex is against the traditional values. Male celibacy and female virginity before marriage was considered attractive. In U.S.A. people being more practical, the stress on virginity has gone. A young man inexperienced in matters of sex would be held not ready for marriage. The girls indulge in plural dating since they want to choose the most compatible mate and the boys willingly comply simply to gain clean experience. Later in Washington I met a girl in late twenties who had become so cynical as to take one into her confidence and show a rack full of neckties from her ex-boy-friends. The girls from Catholic families were more tradition bound and averse to pre-marital sex unless they could be assured of eventual marriage. The girls from split families were keen not to make a mistake in their choice and would be game even for a trial marriage. The American teachers are quite the faculty in the class room, but they are friends outside. Once discussing the qualities to be stressed in the choice of a girl for marriage, the famous Nobel Laureate Prof. R.P. Feynman corrected my simple formula. I was keen for pretty face and cultured conversation reflecting good education and family exposure. According to him the most desirable qualities in a wife should be devotion and kindness which are genuine personality attributes and not just acquired often superficially. Love no doubt is a spur to one's character and potential. There is need for a delicate balance between aggression and submission. The drab winter scene without any visible life and the snow hanging from eaves and trees, could seem most picturesque when observed through the eyes of love.

After the completion of my University studies I was keen to meet a suitable girl for marriage. The few Indian girls that were to be seen in Washington were either in the States for keeps or were returning to India shortly and would consider marriage proposals through their family in India. I did not visualise an American wife to have an enjoyable existence in India for long. My own picture of India was rather grim and I could not foresee the tremendous modernization it has managed in the next forty years. On the whole I still hugged my traditional values. I did not have rhythm that spontaneously breaks into dance and music. I could rhyme and converse and could easily succeed in marriage if I were minded to spend my remaining career in the west. Also many times I had held forth for arranged marriage in India when it was criticised by all and sundry at that time. There has been a welcome change and now the talk shows are full of opportunities and problems of self-arranged marriages. In the Indian style arranged marriage after the war, the ultimate decision is very much left to the young folk who may decide after one or two usually chaperoned meetings. The families however undertake to consider a number of proposals and go into all kinds of detail if they so want. Wrong choices inevitably occur, but these are fewer because the families are not blinded by own youth or love and the young folk are attuned for a life-long relationship. The divorce though permitted is not common. A Korean friend at Washington invited us to his marriage feast with an American girl staying close to the International Student House. Next day we were to condole with him because his day old marriage had broken down and the bride had divorced him claiming incompatibility.

I did go steady with a girl friend at Washington who was from a split family. Her mother and an old maid aunt lived in Atlantic city where she had property. I spent couple of week-ends at this sea-side resort with them. She had earlier gone to school in Philadelphia and soon an old friend of hers made up to her, and she preferred to stay on in USA and not to seek her fortune with me in the distant land of India.

Within a few months of my arrival in India, I secured a good government job in Delhi and my value in marriage market was high. Many friends and relatives automatically became match makers. I had brief meetings with about a dozen probables in Delhi as well as outside. I waited till I could meet a girl of my dreams. When through the suggestion of a friend I did encounter her, I waived all suggestions for further meetings since I was afraid that I may not slip from her estimation from her inexperience or from my professions of devotion. On the other hand I had full confidence that we will be quite compatible and an ideal married couple. I had already beheld all virtues in her and have not repented since I was keen on marrying a beautiful girl and she was it. We were married in November 1952. After spending one year at Cochin I was promoted back to Delhi where we stayed until my transfer to Kanpur in 1961. All my three children were born at Delhi. The year after marriage was spent in Cochin and the life at the Naval base was most enchanting with a palatial house, scenic beauty of the Kerala backwaters, an interesting research and management job all contributed to my happiness. The speedy promotion and return to Delhi as the Scientific Adviser to the Navy added to our happiness.

Marriage in India is around ancient customs and rituals. The bridegroom comes in a procession dressed as a warrior with a sword at his side and mounted on a mare. There is a brass band playing popular happy tunes and usually some boys and girls of the wedding party dance impromptu in front of the procession. On the arrival of the procession, there is a ritual welcome with presents for the leading members of the groom's party, and mutual garlanding of the bride and the groom. Then there is a sumptuous wedding feast and afterwards the marriage ceremony where with the guidance of the priest the marriage vows are exchanged between the bride and the groom and the priest enumerates new duties and responsibilities to the newly-weds. Hindus legally can have only one wife. But traditionally plural wives are possible but not common. I have come across only one official with two wives living peacefully together. The husband has to have special skill and substance that the two wives live in peace. There is a joke that one with two wives speedily gets bald, since the elder wife plucks out his black hair and the younger one his white hair.

As soon as I joined the Defence Science Organization in January 1952, I teamed up with Dr. Gurbakhsh Singh who had also been a government scholar and was at Harvard. He had returned much earlier but was still awaiting call for a job. He had just been appointed a special research officer at the National Physical Laboratory for chemical research. We rented a house close to the laboratory and awaited developments regarding marriages of both. I got married earlier and immediately the cook left us since he did not want the supervision by the lady of the house. Earlier another servant had decamped with our valuables including my gold medal from student days at Lahore and a gold Sigma XI key that I had got from Cornell. There have been off and on numerous cases of burglary and mayhem due to household servants. My wife has for long time preferred to get service from part-time servants who do not stay on the premises. I stayed in Delhi for about a year and when the Naval laboratory at Cochin had occupied its temporary premises and the British commandant of the Naval base at Cochin assured me married accommodation from the Naval officers quota as a special favour for starting scientific work for the Indian Navy there, I moved with my wife to Cochin. In the meanwhile Dr. Gurbakhsh Singh had also married and when I returned to Delhi on promotion, we again could manage to rent a double apartment house for both our families. We stayed together practically like brothers till he moved to Hoshiarpur as a Professor of Chemistry in the Government College there. He later moved to Varanasi and then retired as the Vice-Chancellor of the Delhi University. His wife became a well known musician and professor of Music and is still teaching music at the Delhi University. They, however, were not blessed with any children, but both husband and wife have enjoyed their extremely busy lives.

At Cochin we were practically playing house. Our house was at the head of the Naval anchorage with boats plying between Naval jetty and Ernakulam, the main city across the harbour. Every evening my wife would remember that some minor thing was missing like salt or matches and off we went by boat to the city and came back at dinner time. The servants in the base were reliable and security cleared. From our windows, we could see the skeleton crews at work on the Naval ships at anchor and were often invited on board. After my move to Delhi next year, I visited Cochin almost every few months for progressing the research projects in the Naval laboratory or on ships. My wife liked the scenery and the sunsets of Kerala and later made a special effort to visit the rest of the State of Kerala as house guest of some friends from Kanpur going there to attend a marriage.

The memorable occasions at Delhi were the births of my children, an invitation visit to the Scripps Institute of Oceanography and Conferences in London, Ottawa and Copenhagen already mentioned earlier. I also attended the IUGG General Assembly at Helsinki after visiting Oslo. As a part of this visit I cherish the visit to Moscow and the overflight over the high Himalayas to which I shall return in a later chapter. I have mentioned earlier my return to the student's desk at the National Defence College. As a bonus for returning to studies, the college gave us full one month's vacation with considerable home work involving reading of interesting books on planning and development, etc. This was the only occasion I could spend few weeks of summer on the hill resort of Mussoorie. At the Indian hill resorts in summer the atmosphere is of perpetual fair ground. The recreation industry is supreme. There are horseback rides for children, souvenir hunting for ladies, housie and gambling games for the rich, and treks and picnics everyday.

We had already moved into official accommodation in Delhi and my wife had the advantage that her parents and brothers were in the neighbourhood. I was often away on duty and on tour. The National Defence College took us around to visit most of the cultural and industrial centres besides the security oriented tours of borders and military displays. We could visit as a part of the course, the famous Vishwa Bharati University set up by Rabindranath Tagore at Shantiniketan, the Tata Steel Works at Jamshedpur, a colliery in the neighbourhood, Vrindaban Gardens at Mysosre along with famous south Indian temples and defence establishments around Bangalore, Hyderabad and Poona. We combined the air displays at Agra along with a visit to the Taj. We could accomplish all this because the first course had been for fifteen months duration without a foreign tour, while the courses later were only of one year including the foreign tour. In those days there was a family lunch in the College every Saturday when the wives could also join. Whenever in Delhi, we have enjoyed attending their annual get together on the foundation day in April.

The move to Kanpur was very congenial for the bringing up and the initial education of my children. They all claim to belong to Kanpur where they spent their childhood. My daughter completed her high school plus two there and then competed for joining the IIT, Delhi where she completed her five years M.S. course in Mathematics and became an accomplished operational researcher and software expert. After few years she got married to an NRI physician in U.S.A. She used her qualifications and experience with the Hindustan Computers of Delhi in a job with a famous American computer firm but resigned when she had to look after her infant daughter and found that because of the earnings of her husband, her own salary was practically taken away by the tax man. My daughter has exceptional abilities. Not only did she top the list of successful candidates in the IIT, but also she had talent and qualifications in music and dance. She did not have the occasion to display her talents in U.S.A., but in India she often gave performances in drama, concert or the Delhi Choir. Anyway, her daughter is a budding piano player and among the 15 best students of her age in U.S.A. in a recent competition. Her son is already showing precocious interest in Golf inherited, I suppose from his father. He once dazzled his school inspector when he replied without batting an eyelid that there were twelve seconds in a year. When asked to explain he rattled off the twelve months that each have a second day of the month.

After high school, my daughter got a University scholarship tenable for two years, but strange were the ways of Indian socialism those days, she got the scholarship for one month and a certificate that she had won the University scholarship for two years. The rest of the money went to make up the State deficit especially because she came from a better off family. Thus the climate is not for nourishing talent but suppressing it if it is seen in a well-to-do family.

My elder son, younger than the daughter by three years was once hailed by a friend whose hobby was fortune telling that he has the special favour of the gods and will accomplish almost impossible tasks like stepping on the moon for example. An American had just done so on behalf of all mankind. My son Dinesh has already been to Antarctica in an Indian expedition on behalf of the Indian Oil and Natural Gas Commission which he serves as an exploration Geo-physicist. He is the smartest of my three children with an enormous capacity to make friends and garner knowledge of all kinds from all sources. He inspires confidence and many of his friends load him with various tasks with the firm conviction that he will deliver the goods. He is married to a smart Karnataka girl whom he met during the Antarctica expedition, she being also a member of the same expedition. She, besides being a civil engineer has obtained the M.Tech. degree in electronics and is employed by the Tata Consultants. They have also two children: a very smart youngster and a quiet daughter studying in school at Bombay.

My younger son Rajesh took to medical education by choice even when he was offered an alternative choice of a talent search scholarship for agricultural sciences. He has obtained his master's degree in surgery from Ludhiana Christian Medical College and was engaged in medical research at the All India Institute of Medical Sciences, Delhi. Luckily in the lottery of arranged marriages, he has married a wife who complements him in certain ways. She is a good housekeeper. She has egged him on to try his best to emigrate to U.S.A. where they place more value on experienced medical doctors than they do in India. Now the husband and wife with their baby girl are in the U.S.A. where Rajesh has secured a three year employment visa for a medical research job and has applied for the coveted green card. I expect a great future there or anywhere for their baby girl, who is already winning admirers in the department stores of Boston and vicinity where her parents go for shopping. Rajesh has cultivated his interests in photography and computers.

Now is the time to express my admiration and appreciation for all that my wife has done for her family and me. She had been the anchor around which the family has flourished. At start she had studied at the Miranda House and later after marriage graduated from Punjab University. She was one of the most beautiful girls on the campus and was the cover girl of the popular Caravan magazine. She came from a traditional Punjabi family of Jalandhar which had moved to Delhi on the transfer of her father from West Punjab on the partition of India. She had integrated religious views since the father was an active Arya Samajist and the mother a Sanatanist. She is too rational to go for any demonstration of worship and heart wringing before God or his idols. But she is considerate for human suffering and was the court of appeal of many employees of government wherever I was working and would help them get redress. She is fond of gardening and travel. Under her guidance, the gardens attached to our offices and residences got coveted first prizes in the competitions. She loves to cook for the family and has the insight into what is good for whom. Her entertainment of guests is lavish. Her writing and descriptions of sights is poetic and is easily publishable.

Having become the first lady in the small scientific communities, she has developed a knack of winning people's confidence at all levels. One woman doctor complained to her about her scientist husband. She discovered that he mistreated her on account of wrong understanding of the famous texts on love. It was written that the love exists with fear and went about making his wife afraid of him. The text actually means that the lover has fear of getting rebuffed by the beloved, but the scientist husband was too mulish to understand and soon got divorced. Both of them are happily married again and I suppose he understands the aphormism better. My wife often relates an eye-opener anecdote about her misplaced consideration of a sweepress who complained that her husband who was a government employee had vanished leaving no trace and she was reduced to be a pauper. By her intervention a son was given a government appointment which could be done in case of a scheduled caste employee's distressed family. As soon as couple of months elapsed, before the services of the absconding employee could be terminated, lo and behold, he was back to occupy his job.

Our part-time gardener had a philosophical streak like the famous Do-Little of Bernard Shaw's Pygmalion. One of his complaints was that those who borrow are keen to forget that deal, but the lenders do not ever forget. After some drinking of neat alcohol, he would wax eloquent and comment critically on government rules and routines. According to him the best job in the world was that of a government paid night watchman, which he himself occupied. One should sleep on the job and earn extra money in day time. One is inclined to believe that most security jobs are sinecures from the amount of scams, swindles and pilfering that goes on including travelling without proper tickets, sale at profit of cinema and cricket game tickets, etc., etc. I am sure India will go for automation more earnestly in order to escape further attentions of low paid employees. Clever and workaholics among our people will be programmers and engineers for production and repairs of the automatic machines. The excess production then could support the mass of the people in their lethargy and leisure for the Utopia of total welfare!

I myself belong to the Nanda sub-caste of the Hindu Khatris of the Punjab. Research has shown that most such sub-castes in the Punjab have names that reproduce the names of villages or geographical features in Georgia supporting the theory that in ancient times certain European tribes migrated eastwards. Some of our customs smell of ancestor worship common with the central Asian tribes and the belief in a benign God who often incarnates in human form for the uplift of the human race is also traceable to central Asia who initiated the Mahayana form of Buddhism incorporating caring pantheon of Boddhisattvas to whom one could pray. The incarnations of Vishnu serve the same purpose. My mother hailed from a Bedi family and thus was a descendent of Guru Nanak and most Bedis believe that they have inherited traces of spirituality from Guru Nanak to this day. She believed that she often got premonition of future happenings

Dr. J.N. Nanda and Mrs. Chander Kanta at their marriage in 1951

(L-R) Mr. Rajendra with Mr. Baikunth Nath Nanda,
elder brothers of the author

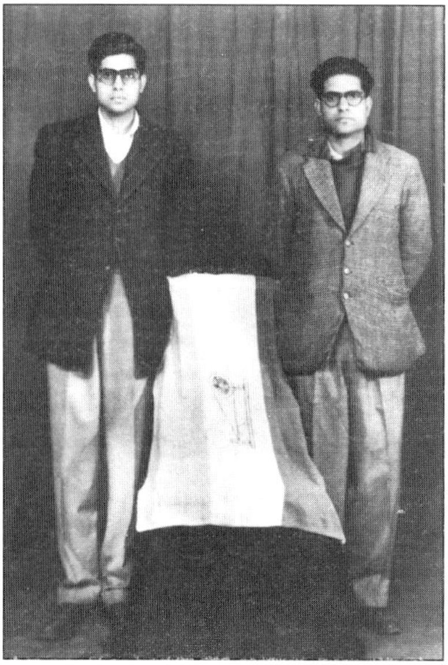

Author with his elder brother Mr. Rajendra in 1945 on his release from Multan Jail

Family photo on the marriage of author's niece Dr. Prem Lata Chawla. Author's brother Principal Kidar Nath with his wife is at extreme Left

Author's two children, Dinesh and Rajesh in 1942

Author's daughter, Shashi in her dance costume at Kanpur

Author's daughter, Shashi with her husband Dr. Raj Chawla

Downwind Expedition, 1958. [Back row, L to R: Robert M. Norris (shading eyes with hand), Robert H. Parker (in large hat). Front row L to R: Dr. J.N. Nanda, Indian Navy, unidentified crewman, Bos'n Clyde Rice (with bongo drums), John Andrews, M.D. (UK), Maxwell Silverman (in pith helmet), Dr. Robert L. Fisher (seated wearing large hat), Robert O. Pepin (seated) and Russell W. Raitt (standing)]

Author with his class fellows and faculty at National Defence College, Delhi (1961)

Author with the Defence Minister at Defence Laboratory, Kanpur

Mrs. Nanda receiving best Garden Prize from the Defence Minister at Kanpur

Defence Material Research Laboratory at Kanpur (1966)

Author at the convocation of Institute of Armament Technology, Pune

Author with the Vice Chancellor (centre)
Harvard University, Boston (2008)

Author and his daughter with Prof. Fred Singer at Cosmos Club, Washington D.C.

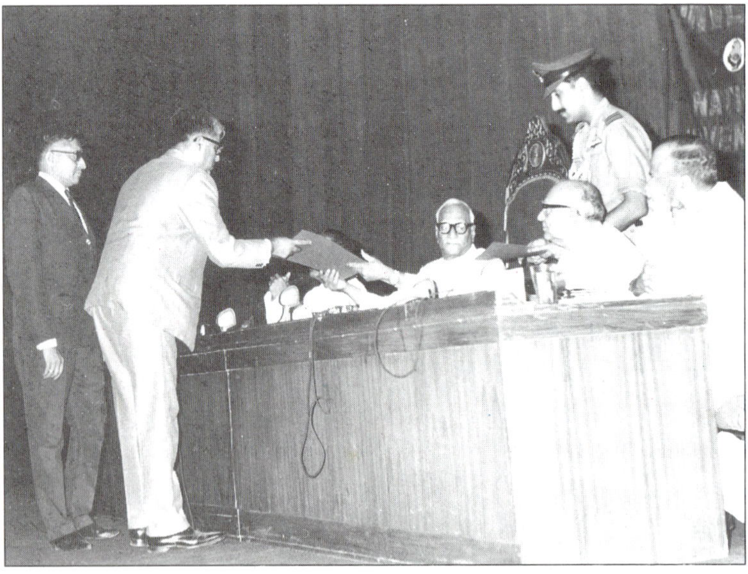

Dr. J.N. Nanda receiving Invention Promotion Award at Vigyan Bhawan, New Delhi (1970)

VIII

Kanpur

In June 1961, I reached Kanpur, Shri B.S. Deugen, the Dy. Director had written to me that I would be temporarily accommodated with the Station Staff Officer until they could allot a suitable accommodation in the cantonment which was considered to be the most liveable area for the defence scientists. Within a short while I was allotted a nice hutment next to the Kanpur Club which we used almost like an extension of our house. The club had all the usual facilities like the swimming pool and cards rooms, etc. And it was not very much frequented by the members, I gathered, because of the enforcement of the dry laws. Close by were the schools for the girls and the boys. Shashi joined the St. Mary's Convent High School and the boys the Methodist High School after their nursery classes in other schools. Later the boys shifted to the Central School since for the children of the Central Government officers, the central schools are more convenient as the syllabus and teaching are uniformly of a high standard all over India and admission is guaranteed if the parents move on official transfer. Kanpur is in the middle of the northern cultural belt of India. There are many institutions of song and dance. Shashi chose to learn music and dance in the evenings and by the time she passed the high school plus two, she had also graduated in Kathak dance and in classical music.

So far the primary function of the laboratory had been to keep specifications for all materials up-to-date and to carry out quality control of all defence supplies coming in their purview. A year earlier some staff had been earmarked in each division for R & D work and soon after my reaching there, the separation of research and inspection staff was completed. Later the inspection staff entirely separated into an inspectorate of materials. We did not cover metals or textiles. The equipment and plant facilities for inspection and research were usually common under the same Assistant Director or division head. A separate Dy. Director looked after the inflow of inspection work and sent scientists for inspection and like duties. The level of intake in the laboratory had been rather low and so most of the staff were only graduates in science and hoped to rise in research and inspection jobs by time scale. I explained to the staff that the merit of a scientist will be determined by the quality of creative work carried out by him and it would be easier to prove themselves in R & D than in inspection where bulk of the work would be routine testing to specifications. They have to work closely together since new materials will mean new specifications and coining new tests which may be simpler or more efficient, will also be termed R&D work. There was announcement of a new policy for inspection ushered in by the U.S. National Bureau of Standards. They had found that rather than reach the merit dictated by various tests, it was easy to reach the performance of an acceptable supply. They termed it testing to the quality of a reference material. We had considerable difficulty in import substitution of the fire-fighting foam compound from U.K. So we geared up to set up performance tests and to match the laboratory performance with that of an imported sample but later we discovered that the entire exercise was futile since the imported British sample was only a deteriorated version of the store as it had taken about two years after production to reach us. The fire-fighting compound deteriorates to about 50 per cent efficiency in the process and such a sample cannot be a reference sample. This study had one good result. At least defence indenters stopped swearing by the British imported product and were more content with the quality verdict of the laboratory. I had a better experience with Russian imports since from the very beginning they accepted our view on quality of materials and whenever there was some doubt and the Indian indenters raised questions with the Russian suppliers, they invariably asked them to route the enquiry through us in case we also wanted some clarification.

The laboratory had prepared a number of required stores like greases, oils, lubricants, additives, protectives, etc., and could pass on the know-how. But unfortunately private industry required large and guaranteed repeat orders, while the defence requirements were small and occasional. For meeting urgent wartime requirements, the laboratory set up a production division in order to make supplies on pilot plant or even laboratory scale basis. Jawaharlal Nehru praised in Parliament the efforts of the laboratory in the supply of engine starting aid in the Himalayan cold that kept the army vehicles moving in the absence of battery heating and shelters for vehicles. After the Chinese conflict, the production division was disbanded, but on account of persistent demand from army indenters for new stores offered by the laboratory for their user views, the scientists in the laboratory organized a cooperative production society from their personal funds and spare time after office hours. The society supplies included de-ionized water for aircraft fuel, lipsalve for cracking of lips in extreme cold, volatile corrosion inhibitor and volatile fungal inhibitive papers for packing and storing, some greases and other specialty items especially for cleaning guns and descaling of engines, etc. The society was found very useful just after the disbanding of the production division. It is highly recommended that every major laboratory should have a production division attached to it for batch production of new innovative items not only for proving but also for offering the items for large scale user trials and the production division can then also encourage private industry to reserve some capacity for experimental production of new items which are likely to be required in bulk later on. I found that really new concoction of composite items like greases and lubricants, drugs and anti-oxidants cannot be made by just following written formula by the industry since each component item has to be of a set quality and ingredients. Industrial production invariably flounders in such new items by relying on their own ingredients and short cuts. The development laboratory's supervision is essential for initial production before one can safely trust the production to be established.

The laboratory was very much involved with storage stability and service life of stores and, therefore, dealt with packaging aids and environmental degradation in a big way. We had a tropical room, exposure ranges at Kanpur, Jodhpur, and Tezpur in three distinct climatic open spaces. Treatments of textiles were tested under exposure to various fungi. The fungal collection of the laboratory was included in the list of world microbiological collections. The division of physical chemistry besides dealing with theoretical understanding of the corrosion process, was engaged in corrosion prevention and anti-corrosion devices including cathodic and anodic protection. A section dealt with development of paints with special properties in infrared, etc. The Petroleum Products division had been keeping up-to-date with laborious engine tests of fuels and lubricants. They were also making a success in import substitution regarding fuels and lubricants for newly acquired Russian equipment. The Soviet authorities were quite satisfied with our efforts in import substitution since it reduced their commitments and they even advised the Indian indentors to get our advice before raising demands with them.

Environmental degradation and its prevention was a chief occupation of this laboratory. Textile treatments, painted surfaces, lubricants, drugs and antibiotics all suffered degradation from oxidation, sunlight and from fungi. The laboratory kept adding to its collection of fungi from all kinds of degraded materials.

The entomology section of the laboratory endeared itself to the services by giving them detailed instructions for fighting the insect infestation menace in their provisions for rations and fodder in the depots and godowns. An inter service Stores Preservation Organization grew up with information cells at all service headquarters treating the Kanpur laboratory as the resource organization. Here was one organization that by its efficiency brought about its end. The preservation instructions have now become the service lore and except for certain periodical preservation refresher courses the organization has no other activity. The laboratory has also shed the entomology section to a field laboratory at Tezpur. In 1972, I got down to visiting the field officer at Western Command who was also the scientific adviser to the command and had assisted in many user trials. We were interested in direct user comments on the recent trial supplies of lip salve and the boreclap, a gun cleaning compound.

This visit took me to the borders with Tibet and then separately by flight from Chandigarh to Leh for Ladakh. I visited units guarding the heights beyond Leh. The severity of the climate has to be experienced and is impossible to describe. Since I did not have proper acclimatization routine I experienced like other newly entering people the acute mountain sickness after first hectic few days filled with exhileration, meetings and visits and curtailed my stay after official work to the bare minimum to catch the flight back. The jawans on high pickets also manage to locate springs in caves for their customary morning bath. In Ladakh in the absence of flowers, hand carved stones are placed as offerings to the guardian deities of the village one might visit. Round about Leh are located some ancient monasteries with their treasures of religious scrolls and paintings.

We held a national symposium on corrosion and later a commonwealth corrosion symposium in which it was decided to regard the Kanpur laboratory as the commonwealth clearing house for all corrosion related information. The closing function of the symposium was attended also by the Scientific Adviser to the U.S. President. It was later that the area of corrosion was recognised as of prime importance for the saving of world resources of metals. Just after the India Pakistan war of 1965 when Pakistan was to decide to leave the commonwealth, there was convened the Commonwealth Defence Science Advisory Committee's conference on clothing and general stores in Australia. I was sent as leader of the delegation of two with Col. Hussain, the chief inspector of general stores, Kanpur. The conference was of one month's duration. My reaction was that this was too long a time for a technical conference and I recommended that future conferences should be limited to ten days duration leaving it to individual delegates to extend their programme by mutual arrangement with the hosts. The recommendation was adopted later for future conferences. We had an excellent stay in Melbourne and on week-ends had sight-seeing trips to resorts in the neighbourhood. The peculiar fauna and flora of Australia was beyond normal experience in other countries just as the southern sky had different view with the pride of place being occupied by the southern cross and not the pole star. The trees in Australia often secrete gums that might assist the breeding of flies. Along with sheep farms all over the countryside, the summer there is the season of flies more than the summer in plains of India. I visited Sydney and Canberra. An air force officer took me for a flight over the city in his private aircraft. The chief point of the conference was the demonstration of recent advances in the design and development of clothing and tentage by Australia which possibly could be exported to other commonwealth countries.

On the way to Australia, we could spend couple of days in Singapore and while returning we had couple of nights stay at Hong

Kong. These visits were very entertaining as to trade emporia. The products of all lands are available in these cities often at prices less than the price in the countries of origin. I made purchases of some household gadgets and clothes at both the places. In my official report I suggested that India should also have a display of Indian manufactures in Australia since that seemed to be a growing market untouched by Indian capabilities, while China was making efforts to enter it. Australia was also making progress in deep sea fishing and would like to consider India as a future market for their sea catch.

In 1968, I was invited to participate in a symposium on corrosion and modelling of climates at Prague by the Czechoslovakia National Academy of Sciences. All the participants were housed in the same castle where the symposium sessions were held and there was easy access for mutual discussions. I could see the laboratories of Dr. Richtera, the authority on modelling of climates. The Czechs were exporting machines and goods to every corner of the earth and naturally the industry there wanted the equipment to be proofed for the weather of the user country. This was the spur to their researches on modelling of climates especially since theirs was a small country and not extending over vast area covering many climatic zones like India, the commonwealth or the United States. In an extension of this visit I spent few days at the Institute of Petroleum in France and the Rubber Technology section of the Imperial College, London, since we were developing such sections in the Kanpur laboratory further.

A number of doctorate research problems were being tackled. One scholar worked on the inertial system of sea currents. Another on the effect of positive ions in the semi-conducting properties of silver chloride crystals. Another student grew successfully the sapphires and studied the effect of slight impurities. Dr. Y.L. Arora of Wissitex fame was one of these students. We were successful in solving a long standing problem of forecasting the proneness to corrosion from the meteorological factors governing the climate. The paper published in the British Corrosion Journal was highly appreciated and proved to be the culmination of all such efforts. An interesting set of experiments sought to distinguish thorns from the crystallinity therein. This has a bearing on how sharp cutting edges are created. I worked out a quantum mechanical theory for the gravitational red shift which has the potential to be applied further in astro-physics. We had to cap our programme of making silicones and surrender it to the scientists in the N.C.L. who were at that time in the initial stages of this effort, while we had already prepared pilot plant scale products and were poised to carry out industrial scale chromatographic separation of silicone mixtures. The Defence scientists at Kanpur did get to grips with important problems on the bench. I believe if scientists are given facilities and broad objectives, there will be ample and rewarding success for the country. They also produced carbon fibres for the first time in India.

Most important step is to extract the best effort from the scientific workers by providing proper assistance, comfort and incentives. We managed to do this when very few among our workforce had joined us after obtaining Ph.D. degrees. The laboratory was affiliated to most all the universities as a recognized research institution. The library had excellent stock of books, journals and reports. Most authorities in various subjects exchanged reprints with us. The in-house journal was receiving attention from international abstracting journals. Here too, since the success of the journal was not planned from Delhi and was standing in the way of plans of issuing journals from central offices, we had to cease publication. But by that time I had already left Kanpur and no one was there to point out the pointlessness, rather the harm such ceasing of publication will do to the creative efforts of scores of science graduates. The journal had been published for more than twelve years at no cost and no loss basis. It was started in lieu of the publication of quarterly reports which we curtailed to a mid-year and an annual report only.

The laboratory administration was democratic and responsive. There were certain undercurrents in the beginning of authoritarian regimes in certain sections and too much bureaucratic rule waving. This was countered by instituting a separate section in the annual confidential report of each scientist where he could give his comments on the decisions of his superior officer in confidence. The laboratory encouraged participative entertainment by the staff. We had a cultural society as well as an Indian orchestra. They gave performances not only on the campus but also outside. The Kanpur Science and Technological Society staged technical lectures, displays and open houses, etc. in cooperating institutions. A memorable single day excursion was to the Khajuraho temple complex. The bus had to be ferried across on the way. These temples are world famous for the skill in stone carving and are full of erotic sculptures on the sides of the temple and the towers. These temples reflect the times in the ninth and the tenth centuries when the apex of the religious fervour and the worldly prosperity occurred together in India. Pilgrims and Indian settlers from abroad were routinely visiting this place at that time.

The mistake of declaring the laboratory as a factory which was rectified much later led to trade unions and interference by political parties in the real or imaginary disputes created on account of the inflationary pressure on the workforce even when many welfare measures existed like free dispensaries, ration shop, defence canteen store shop, workers managed canteen, annual clearance sale of used articles of staff households under an exchange bazaar scheme, etc. The laboratory boasted of a tennis court and an open air stage for cultural programmes and plays.

We carried out some experiments on the visco-elastic fracture of plastics and worked out the statistical theory of plastic behaviour. I must record my appreciation of the extreme kindness of Prof. P.J. Flory who took the trouble to explain some of the intricate calculations he had published in Polymer Physics. An important result was the development of "Carbene Rubber" a restructuring of the rubber molecule to build-in the fire resisting property. The new material was expected to be better than the nitrile rubber. The process is patented by the laboratory and deserves the attention of some industry for better rubber tyres of military vehicles since most vehicles catch fire through the rubber tyres in the battle situation.

I had kept track of the International Indian ocean expedition by attending various preparatory and results symposia in Delhi, Waltair, or Goa. In a visit to Kanpur, the manager of the Indian Oil Corporation invited my wife and me to visit Karnataka and he would be glad to provide a guide with a car for brief visits to some fabled landmarks like the Gomateshwar, Halebid and Belur, and the Vrindavan Gardens. My friend Air Marshal Virk from the National Defence College days was at that time posted at Bangalore. We went to Mysore in connection with a scientific meeting and from there we used the Indian Oil hospitality for these visits terminating at Bangalore from where we returned to Kanpur by train. I shall be describing some of these monuments in a subsequent chapter. These wonders are unique and are to be seen to be believed.

A memorable friendship grew with Shri Raj Kumar an ex-Kakori case revolutionary and a colleague of the famous revolutionary Chandrasekhar Azad. It was a pleasure to hear him tell of his anecdotes about Bhagat Singh and his colleagues who often stayed in Kanpur. My brother, the Congress revolutionary also visited me those days and was very happy to meet Shri Raj Kumar and talk about other leaders and old political controversies. I came to know Raj Kumar when he had not yet accepted the stipend being awarded by government to political sufferers, and was in need of some steady income. I had been thinking of having classes in Russian in the laboratory so that some enthusiastic scientists could learn an important foreign language very much involved with our research work. About twenty students joined his Russian class. He was a very good teacher and carried on with this work till he died from fever a couple of years before I left Kanpur. His funeral procession was very large. So many people joined to pay their last respects to a valiant freedom fighter. One of his old colleagues sounded the traditional bugle calls with the funeral procession. Raj Kumar was extremely talented. He once demonstrated proper vocal timbre in music to my daughter who was learning music. Besides classical music, he was an adept in Yoga and from deep study had mastered the ups and downs of communism in Russia. He considered the Chinese to be better revolutionaries as well as more trustworthy. This was inspite of the India-China conflict of 1962 which he assigned to accidental misunderstandings. Raj Kumar, expressed a desire to see snow since he did not know if he would have another chance. In the month of January there is usually snow to be seen in Ranikhet. I drove up to Ranikhet and beyond about 500 kms from Kanpur, but as fickle as the weather the snow was not to be seen that weekend at all. The children enjoyed Raj Kumar's presence in the trip. He had earlier given me very rare knowledge about ancient history and archeology of Kanpur. The suburb Jajmau, he explained, reflected the ancient-most Dravidian occupation as Mau is a Dravidian word. He showed us certain large foundation bricks uncovered by the cutting edge of the river Ganges which from their size were obviously Harappan. At a cut of the river just by the side of the golf course, he showed in embedded pots some ancient pot burials which according to him were pre-Harappan. With the passing away of Raj Kumar a breed of Indian intellectuals is vanishing. In a later visit I found the pots have been shattered by the weather.

Kanpur boasts of a very beautiful Modern Hindu temple. There are memorials scattered around to the martyrs of 1857. The capital city of the Marathas in the north, seat of Nana Fernavis, was Bithur on the western outskirts of Kanpur, and pitched battles were fought there. The wharf and the well where many British soldiers were killed, were regarded as places of pilgrimage for all new entrants to the British officer ranks in India. There is a famous church in the cantonment near our house which was very well furnished with mutiny memorabilia and was architecturally a great monument. Tantia Tope memorial has been erected in the park near the mutiny memorial well. Some of the outstanding scientists in this laboratory were Dr. B. Sanyal and Dr. K.J. Balakrishna, they retired later after becoming directors of the laboratory for short periods. Dr. L.M. Pande and Dr. A.C. Joshi had developed the fireproof rubber and they rose to eminent positions in the Department of Science and Technology and the Institute of Petroleum respectively.

It appeared that the days of innovative directors was coming to a close. There were new many able scientists and the leadership was with the bureaucratic scientist who would work less but talk more and seem useful to the politicians. I was told that a difficult situation had arisen at the Institute of Armament Technology, Pune due to differences in perception of its role and if I would like to take over this institute as administrative as well as teaching head, I readily agreed and became the Director and Dean of the IAT, Pune from 1st January, 1973. I adopted this title to reflect the increased responsibility of the head of this institute in order to carry out better the instructions from both the DRDO and the service chiefs.

Throughout my stay at Kanpur, there were repeated attacks on India in 1956 and 1965 and then again in 1972, by Pakistan besides the attack by China in 1962. What had gone wrong with India's declared aims to live in peace with its neighbours. Though the great war ended in 1945, the world was still not reconciled to peaceful coexistence. A country that favoured solution of international problems by peaceful negotiations was taken to be weak and ready to be bullied given the existence of a bully. There was actually no intention or preparation by India to tread on the toes of its neighbours. There was a unilateral cry from Pakistan, that India was not reconciled with the creation of an independent Pakistan, inspite of repeated assurances to the contrary in words and in actions. Similarly India had tried its level best to befriend and reassure the Chinese that India had no imperial pretensions regarding their suzerainty over Tibet, by surrendering any extra territorial responsibilities regarding that country inherited from the British rulers. China had in the meanwhile started making territorial claims and cartographic aggression against India, besides nibbling silently at the Indian territory claimed by them in Aksai Chin. This led to a toughening attitude regarding the defence of own borders by India but without real military strength or preparedness. This was the situation when China called the bluff in the Indian statements of occupying their own territory up to the stated Mac Mahon line established by treaty between the British and the authorities in Tibet. In addition China was suspicious of the cooling of its relations with the Soviet Union and warmer relations between India and the Soviet Union. In these circumstances they wanted to bully India into compliance by a speedy campaign in the Himalayas. But soon they realized the folly of occupying more Himalayan empty territory without seeing any sign of wavering determination of India to defend her claims. In any case soon there was a unilateral ceasefire and the two countries have not completely left the incident at their back. The border has yet to be mutually agreed, but there is recognized trust for peaceful coexistence and mutual regard on both sides. India is quite convinced that continued cooperation and more trust between India and China will work for the stability of Asia.

Indo-Pakistani conflicts can be understood somewhat in the historical perspective particularly when the viewpoints of the two leaderships of the two countries are rather different. The British Parliament finally carved Pakistan out of colonial India apparently from the democratic wishes of the population of the contiguous areas in the east and the west of India. This is how the British and the democratic leadership of the Indian National Congress that spearheaded the struggle for India's freedom looked at the partition of the country. But on the ground and in the minds of the leadership in the saddle in Pakistan, it was the triumphant conclusion of the vicious hate campaign launched by the Muslim League with the colonial rulers against the National Congress as the party of Indians where majority happened to be non-Muslims. A large majority of Indian Muslims had no such beliefs, nor does the Koran not visualize states where the majority of inhabitants may be non-Muslim. The real guarantee of peaceful life of a citizen is not the rule of his coreligionists, but the rule of law which treats all subject as having the same rights, and does not subscribe to a philosophy of 'us and them'. The majority of Hindus and Muslims thought that in Pakistan, there would be free expression to the Islamic trappings of state while in India the traditional Indian secular state will function dealing justly with all citizens. There was thus a voluntary migration of very few Muslims to the homeland for Indian Muslims which was stated to be Pakistan of the Muslim League's making. The League leadership of free Pakistan could not place limits on their intense propaganda that Muslims cannot live with the Hindus and as soon as the partition was assured, they went about the ethnic cleaning of the Pakistan side of the India's western boundary. Fifty years ago, the population of the Punjab was 40 per cent non-Muslim or Hindus and Sikhs, now they all had to flee with their lives and tales of horror to India. There was spontaneous retaliation in India too but the scale of the holocaust was reduced only by the valiant efforts of the Indian exponents of Hindu-Muslim unity, particularly the Muslim leaders who did not migrate and stayed with the vast masses of Muslim citizens of India. Pakistan's so called fundamentalists called them Indian Muslim nationalist leaders Kafirs or slaves of Kafirs, Kafir being a Koranic term of abuse for those that are apostate Muslims and has naturally no relevance to the views of Hindus or Muslims of India. Not only does Pakistan want itself to be an Islamic state where only Muslims of fundamentalist disposition alone will have all the rights, but they want India to be also a similar state of Hindu fundamentalists so that they can further excite the Indian Muslims to rebel and allow Pakistan to embark on a conquest of India begun a thousand years ago by Islam. It is this insane view for the modern times which is driving the present rulers to acquire by hook or crook the nuclear weapons to subjugate India (and possibly commit suicide in the process). The only remedy lies with the Muslims of Pakistan to face the true face of their rulers and ditch them for saner and genuinely ethical leadership that treats human beings as human beings.

India swears by peaceful co-existence and sorting out of problems by mutual consensus. This requires spirit of compromise and conciliation. India has repeatedly demonstrated this by offering Pakistan very easy terms after repulse of every aggression by them. The whole of J&K is claimed by India. Haji Pir Pass was occupied by Pakistan illegally and they lost it in the 1965 conflict, still India agreed to its adverse possession as a compromise under the advice of the mediators. The 'us and them' grouping sponsored by militant Islam is neither suitable for Muslims of India nor for other Indians. Even after the liberation of Bangladesh with the assistance of the Indian army, India speedily evacuated its army and allowed Bangladesh to have its own political evolution. We regret that they have also belatedly discovered the ruinous road of fanaticism planted by the Pakistan movement in free Bangladesh and are now valiantly struggling to contain it.

At the time of partition of India, the choice to join Pakistan or India was left by the British with the Maharaja or the Indian prince ruling J & K State. He had first made a standstill agreement with both the dominions and probably desired to bargain with both for better terms for merger. Indian leaders made it clear to him that he should have the views of his subjects in mind. The population of J&K was mainly Muslim, but was mainly represented by the Muslim Conference of J&K which soon renamed itself the National Conference of J&K. Sheikh Abdullah was the unquestioned leader of this organization. He was not taken in by the embellishments of the Muslim League and rebuffed the advances made by Mr. Jinnah on behalf of the League in his visit to Srinagar. On becoming independent and Pakistan finding itself controlling about half of the Indian army with the many British officers openly favouring the advancement of Pakistan, the Pakistani leaders tried to force the Maharaja by letting loose a horde of tribal raiders from across Pakistan to loot and occupy J&K territory in the west. The Maharaja was forced to decide but his decision was against Pakistan. He acceded his state to India and begged that it should now be protected from the raiders, which was done. He had also the support of his subjects through the National Conference leadership. Now after considerable preparation and with the connivance of small disgruntled elements, Pakistan has again egged on the Mujahideen of fundamentalist brand and the mercenaries from across its borders to infiltrate into J&K and carry out terrorist attacks against the democratic leadership in the State. This war by proxy is also being squarely met by the J&K citizens and the security forces of India. Now Pakistan is shouting itself hoarse in defence of the human rights of the terrorist attackers ignoring the human rights of the peaceful minorities who have been living in J&K for ages. Already the terrorists have started ethnic cleansing of J&K and many Hindu and Sikh citizens have fled to the neighbouring Indian States. With the connivance of its British officers, the Ladakh Scouts, an armed police raised by the Maharaja, Pakistan quietly annexed northern areas from the State comprising Gilgit, etc. For any future negotiations, Pakistan does not include these areas as negotiable. India has shown great forbearance and offered a compromise to settle for the line of control as the international boundary.

This is entirely wrong to regard such a compromise as a sign of weakness of the India's claims bolstered by the history of full autonomy and repeated elections having been held in the J&K State under Indian jurisdiction. The special autonomous status includes a separate constitution, separate flag and limited acceptance on approval by the State Legislature of Indian inter-State apparatus. It was India which complained to the Security Council that they should get Pakistan to vacate its aggression in the State. The United Nations have passed many resolutions leading to a plebiscite but they also ask Pakistan to first vacate its aggression which they have never begun doing. On the contrary they have encouraged genocide of the religious minorities in J&K. India is at present engaged in overcoming the terrorist menace. After pacification and return of the refugees, free and fair elections under the State Constitution already there for more than forty years, will be held and the State will have a government of their choice. The State Constitution favours religion to be kept apart from politics and human rights. The negotiations if any with Pakistan have to be only to the extent the Pakistan occupied parts will be part of the autonomous secular State or will go their separate ways. Among the Indian held areas, Ladakh and Jammu will have limited autonomy for their development within the J&K State and the Kashmir valley will have a majority in the State Legislature. India on principle, cannot tolerate its own break-up by recognizing a part as sovereign. J&K itself will be a composite nation of diverse languages and faiths as well as diverse terrains. The only way to live a peaceful life will be through secularism and democracy which they can certainly have as an autonomous part of India along with all the benefits that an Indian State has. A third world country cannot progress if it hugs to its bosom the illiterate leadership of dogmatic priests who extols the piety of following the fossilized practices of the past. Kashmir was the cradle of ancestor worship of Hinduism and Buddhism and preached the fellowship of men to distant lands. Some accidents made their ruler a Muslim and then Islam spread by tolerance and mixed doctrines. Only after 1947, due to inattention by the secular forces, the reactionary beliefs have been diligently spread by foreign guns and foreign money. Ethnic aggression offers immediate gains to the local ethnic majority and the Pakistani example encouraged certain religious leadership among the Sikhs to do the same and throw out the non-Sikhs from a small part of the Punjab aiming to convert it into Khalistan. Such logic when accepted by Sant Bhindranwala got a following and there was almost a localized rebellion against the Indian State immediately supported by men, materials, training grounds and sanctuaries by Pakistan in their short-sighted feud against India. With considerable expenditure of energy and organization, the Indians have eliminated the Khalistani terrorists and the local population is back into the secular mainstream.

Pakistan has taken to heart the lesson of History that a small country can overrun a big country, e.g., the early Muslim victories over Persia, the ancient victory of Greece over the Persian empire, etc. They also have learnt that the tenacity of purpose is important and repeated attacks could lead to a freak victory as happened for Robert Bruce of Scotland and for Mohammed Ghauri *vs*. Prithvi Raj of Delhi. But they forget that India has also learnt her lessons of History that enemy has to be defeated to the extent that its leadership no longer poses a threat. Any future attack by Pakistan under some intoxication or the other like that of *Jihad* or confidence in atomic bombs, will be met in such a fashion that aggressive Pakistan is no longer viable. And the successor states will have to agree to believe in democracy and human rights for all irrespective of religion and language. The Sindhis and the Pushtuns are long suffering ethnic minorities there.

India's domestic and foreign policies are well established policies of peace and progress. The Indian leadership was at the forefront of opposition to imperialism, apartheid, colour bar, suppression of the Palestinian state, and for the liberation of Africa. India has a large population in a large country endowed in every way. There are guaranteed human rights irrespective of age or sex. There is freedom of press and information. The state is democratic. They go out of their way to raise the social status and the economic strength of the depressed sections. There is widespread belief in secularism which is not simply respect for all religions and modes of worship, but allows an individual to take pride in being multi-religious and finding no conflict in many gods or none at all. India has contributed liberally to international concerns of security, anti-terrorism, and battle against narcotics and smuggling. They support loyally the U.N. and the regional groupings like the SAARC. India and Pakistan actually cancel each other in world calculations and India would rather want the reverse so that like-mindedness between India and Pakistan will increase the influence of both in world affairs.

Our newspapers and personal experience of many Indians who visit Pakistan point that people to people relations are still excellent when we act from our common culture of ethical life. We are, therefore, prepared to start from a clean slate and forgive and forget the wrongs committed or suffered by our ancestors in this land. We should rather recall the great sacrifices made by all Indians while evolving a common culture, common concept of ethical life and common ambitions for the after life. There are rich poetry and literature from inspired Hindu and Muslim scholars and poets. India wishes to bury the hatchet provided by communal chauvinism, intolerance and aggressive self-estimation, and further build bridges of understanding between India and Pakistan.

India is certain that the future of civilization lies in the evolution of a world culture and a world embracing philosophy. One world could not be established by generals and emperors. But it is possible by recognizing unity in diversity and the belief that diversity leads also to creativity so essential for continued well being of the citizens of the world. Akbar the Great succeeded within India to create a climate of mutual trust and regard between Hindus and Muslims. Our secularism has grown from the ideas of Akbar and Ashoka and modern thinkers like Nehru and M.N. Roy. We also draw on the philosophy of love and tolerance of a number of gifted great men of religion. The Indian secularism respects virtue even when practised by people of other religions or by atheists or the communists. In political theory India believes in democracy, in coexistence and conflict resolution by negotiations. In economics we wish to tread the middle path/private profit tempered with the concern for the poor and universal employment even at the cost of slower production preferring man to machine. Neo-capitalism will require a market based on truth and wider interest than just self-interest.

In the post-industrial phase, India would like to sweep away all cobwebs of history and the dark lanes of dogma that divide man from man and that curtail the human rights of others.

India has only friendship, loyalty and mutual aid in view, for the smaller neighbours as demonstrated by her actions in Bangladesh, Sri Lanka, Nepal, Bhutan and recently in suppressing the coup in Maldives. The same friendship holds for Burma, Singapore, Yemen, Somalia, and the Gulf states. India has had close friendly and religious ties with Saudi Arabia and Thailand. India's support for creation again of the Palestine state has been continuous and the ties with Israel have also improved after the recent accords between Israel and the PLO. We are never happy with growing violence in international relations and tendency to take law in own hands by certain states. India would like the United Nations to be strengthened by involving them deliberately in the resolution of disputes. The Security Council should be more representative and perhaps veto to be effective should be endorsed also by one more permanent member and permanent membership may be increased from the present five to new seven. India hopes to contribute to the security of the Indian Ocean in association with SAARC countries as well as South Africa and Australia and does not see much role for countries not bordering the Indian Ocean in this regard.

In view of India's geographical location and its long coastline, India has to have a strong Navy. India would gladly share the security aspects of the trade routes across the Indian Ocean with other concerned countries, particularly the Arab countries, Iran and Pakistan and such cooperation is bound to increase as these countries shed inhibitions against civilized contacts with non-Muslim and non-fundamentalist regimes as well as agree to work against international terrorism and desist from recruiting or financing terrorists and fanatics for attacks in other countries.

Burma was also at one time a part of greater India primarily through culture and religion and later by the annexation to British India. Many Indians have commercial and business relations with this country and would like to strengthen these further. Netaji's campaign to liberate India was mainly staged in Burma. Burma can always count on partnership for development with India. India would welcome Burma to be member of both the SAARC and the ASEAN groupings which can smooth the feathers all around.

Just as USA sent a man on the moon on behalf of all mankind, India is engaged on deep ocean mining and the exploration of the Antarctica we feel, on behalf of the entire world. Our experience in these border areas of research or in space research is available to all who may benefit from it.

IX

Scenes and Monuments

Most of my travels were incidental to my scientific work apart from few journeys for recreation or social calls. A scene which is imprinted on my memory is of the winding road below when I was going up the Abbotabad climb in west Punjab, now in Pakistan. Suddenly it became also cooler and we seemed to have entered a paradise from the scorching plain below. I was in my late teens when I had a gun pointed at me by a guard of the rail track near Kotri in the Sind province of present Pakistan when I had gone for a morning walk while visiting certain relatives living in the railway quarters at Kotri. I did not realize that the government had been excited by the Hur rebellion in Sind. Longest commercial sea passage I had was on a troop ship just after the war in 1946 from Calcutta to San Francisco with a very brief halt at Shanghai on the way. This is the only time I have been on Chinese soil. Kuomintang was still evidentially in control in 1946. The American troop ship and the troops if any and other passengers on it were treated as friendly visitors. We were allowed ashore with hardly any visa formalities. For couple of nights we were out there, we spent the nights in the comfortable bunks of the ship. In Shanghai I caught sight of a gurudwara pennant and walked up to the gurudwara. It was functioning exactly like a Sikh temple in the Punjab. The granthi (attendant on the Sikh scriptures) was an ex-policeman of the force raised by the British for the defence of the extra-territorial rights of few decades in the past. He was very friendly and enjoyed using his Punjabi in conversation with me. He apparently looked down his lordly nose on the Chinese natives since he was allied to the conquering British. He claimed that the Chinese had no idea of true religion or of God. They worshipped "Bhusa" whose statues were enshrined in their temples. He followed the Chinese reading of the name of Buddha and had no idea of Buddhism as a great religion and its origin in India.

The famous Golden Gate Bridge at San Francisco was very impressive. Now one can see some cracked buildings near the entrance, these cracks have occurred after my first glimpse then. Steeply inclined streets with rickety looking trams were typical of the place. The steepest such streets and a whole community staying on the crags was the fishing village that I visited later on the ocean side of the island of Victoria off the Canadian coast. I broke journey on the train ride to New York to have a look at the Grand Canyon and the Niagra Falls. Both are the "trademark" scenes of U.S.A. One can spend a lifetime in exploring the Grand Canyon. The best view one has of the Niagra falls is from the open deck of the boat that takes you down to the foot of the falls close to the Canadian bank of the river. This close view I had only in 1991 when my son-in-law drove down all the way to Niagra Falls from Boston. We stayed at the famous Holiday Inn on the U.S. side.

For entertainment, shopping paradise and variety in food and fruit, Delhi gets the crown. Every kind of entertainment is available at very small cost. Dance and music programmes are practically free almost for anyone who takes the trouble to reach the site of the programme. There are so many seasonal exhibitions and programmes arranged by the Delhi and the All India Tourism Departments. This is the mango season and they will exhibit all the available three hundred odd mango varieties along with how much can be purchased and where. Same happens in the 'ber' or the apple season. There are innumerable flower shows. We are very fond of dutifully visiting the dahlia and the rose shows in line with ancient interest of my wife who often had first prizes for these as well as for her garden in Kanpur or Pune. In Delhi, we now live in a flat and having a small terrace garden is sufficient problem with the summer shortage of water.

State tourism departments as well as certain tourist agencies provide package tours from one day to a week or more including transportation, hotel accommodation and guided visits to various temples and sites of tourist interest. In May 1994, we took such a tour for one week offered by the Himachal tourism. This tour took us practically to all the well known temples and sites from Pathankot to Simla. There are historic but living temples on this route. The Baijnath temple near Mandi is about a thousand years old at least. It is a small architectural wonder. The fire temple at Kangra is famous as people directly worship the volcanic flame issuing out of some cracks in a pit inside the temple. The Dasehra festival at Kulu is an emporium of Himachal culture. There are folk plays and songs and many deities from all over the State gather for their annual 'conference'. India always had a free and easy way with the pilgrims. Dharamsalas offered free accommodation and bed and breakfast at nominal charge all along the pilgrim route. Such facilities are still there besides the modern hotels for modern tourist-pilgrims.

Once a Yugoslav delegation came to visit the Kanpur laboratory after the Chinese unilateral ceasefire. I took them also to look at the Gwalior branch laboratory where research on certain chemical stores had just been started. From Gwalior I accompanied them to see the Sonagiri hill complex of Jain temples and later the Gwalior fort. The delegates jointly expressed the view that India does not need any export surplus, they should concentrate only on the import of tourists, there is so much here to attract the visitor. India is so full of sacred places, temples and monuments that any logical protection on international initiative would mean that India will have to keep out of all conflicts that could engulf even a part of its territory. The whole country should be declared a sanctuary barred to warlike stores and aggressive attack in the spirit of the ancient Greek sanctuaries.

The best scene of nature that I have seen is not easy to choose. If I have to choose one, I shall unhesitatingly single out the early morning view on a clear day, of the entire set of Himalayan peaks from the window of a plane flying between Delhi and Moscow. I am told that the green flash over the pacific ocean is also a unique sight. It occurred once during my voyage from the Easter Island to La Jolla, but I missed it. Most ocean going vessels traditionally celebrate the crossing of the equator. If the sea is calm and there is relaxed vigil, it includes some horseplay, including being made to jump in the ocean blind-folded. I recalled the location of the dangling iron ladder and soon located it, but before I could place my foot on the bottom rung, a wave made me jump back into the sea with the ladder. It was only after couple of instants of time that I realized that the ladder was acting as a sinker to me, and then I let go and resurfaced when my ship-mates guided me back to the deck of the ship.

There are so many scenic railway journeys in the world. Most railroad journeys in the hills are entertaining. Once when I was travelling by train from Pune to Goa, most of the passengers were attracted by the hills and valleys and forests passing by. A lady could not desist restraining her husband who was repeatedly standing up to peep outside, asking him if he had never seen trees before!

There is in India a toy train from Gwalior to Shivpuri literally set up, over about twenty miles of track along a river valley, as a pastime for the young prince of Gwalior in the century gone by. The narrow gauge trains reaching Simla from Kalka or reaching Darjeeling from Siliguri provide extremely scenic journeys, apart from the attractive destinations. Similarly the bus rides from the plains to Ooty or Kodaikanal are through gardens and pastures. The stunted trees on account of continuous high winds around the southern tip of India, or when travelling to Mandapam from Madurai have their own charm. A boat-ride through Sunderbans and around Calicut for enjoying the view of the mangroves can be quite entertaining.

There is tremendous awakening regarding the preservation of the human heritage and the earth's eco-system through the efforts of the United Nations and the enlightened people all over the world. Among the famous gardens of the world, there are the Kew Gardens of London, the Central Park in New York, Buchart Gardens of Victoria, the State Garden of Oslo more known for the sculptures that abound there, the Shalimar Gardens of Lahore, the Pinjore Gardens of Chandigarh, the Indian garden cities of Chandigarh and Delhi, etc., etc. The Indian movies have lit the Indian screen with the beauty of the Vrindavan Gardens of Mysore. One need not mention spots in the Swiss Alps or in Kashmir when the whole tract is beautiful. In Swiss mountains, now one can hop from one peak to the next by means of ropeways. The train from Lima to Maachu Pichu, the ancient capital of the Incas high up on the mountain has to have supply of oxygen on tap since some passengers may have trouble breathing at those altitudes.

I shall not enumerate the rich and varied exhibits one can see in the many museums. It is difficult to decide which one of the three has the greatest museum: London, Versailles or the Vatican. The treasures of the world are gathered in these. The American museums seemed to be most alive and devising ever new ways to reach the people especially the young ones. I have often seen special exhibits in the Boston museum or the special films of great interest. Particularly the film they have made about the exploration of the Antarctica is so instructive and absorbing besides being full of thrills of escapes from icy graves. The Cairo museum is still full of ancient gold jewellery or their replicas taken from the mummies and the sarcophagi of the Pharaohs and their queens. It appears the craft of the goldsmiths should be the ancient-most fine art. The Indian jewellers excel in this, these days and the Indian export of gold jewellery is of a staggering amount. The museum at Delhi displays Indian crafts well along with the artifacts highlighting the ancient Harappan civilization of India. Many ancient idols and sculptures of India, Greece, Rome or Egypt are now to be seen in museums of the west. Almost any local museum has many paintings and sculptures, terracotta and ancient artifacts to whet the taste of a discriminating tourist or pilgrim. The most unforgettable temple that I have seen is the Jain temple complex at Mt. Abu. It is an epic in marble. One is elevated to view the heavens when one looks up at the carved ceiling of halls and corridors. The stone pillars of the ancient temple at Belur-Halibed seem like the work of lathe machine on wood. I have already mentioned the sex education available from the carvings on the exterior of the Khajuraho temples of Madhya Pradesh. The Buddhist pilgrim circuit in India has received great patronage from the realization that Buddhism approaches humanism without the underpinning of a belief in relationship with a universal God. The eight places a devout Buddhist wishes to visit are the place of birth (Lumbini), Bodh Gaya (and the Bodhi Tree) being the place of enlightenment, Sarnath near Varanasi (first sermon), place of death or Nirvana, Kushinagar, 55 kms from Gorakhpur, and places connected with his works like Sravasti (Gonda district, U.P), Sankasya (Etah district, UP.), Rajgriha and Vaishali (Patna, Bihar). Other Buddhist pilgrim spots are Sanchi, Nalanda, Ajanta caves, and Udaigiri caves near Bhuvaneshwar, Orissa. I have been equally impressed by the living Buddhist temples in China, Japan, Thailand, Sri Lanka and Nepal. Religious places: Hindu, Muslim, or Christian all reflect the same urge of the people to hold on to a redeemer in the moment of crisis. The great mosques of India,

Cairo or Palestine, the cathedrals of London, Paris and Vienna or the churches of Moscow have all received my humble tribute to the devotion of the masses of human beings. The most scientific description of God is the combined urge and wisdom of the mass of the people of any time and clime.

The forts and palaces of Rajasthan, the Rathouses (courts) of central Europe, the Mayor's palaces in Germany and England, each excels the other. The lordly *havelis* of Rajasthan converted now to hotels are the destination of scores of well healed sheikhs of the world with access by the magic carpet of world's airlines. The buffet lunches at the lake-palace hotel of Udaipur are the gourmet's delight. Same must be said about the Smorgesboards of Europe and U.S.A. The grandeur of the city, their bright paint and the picture post card quality of the street corners surpasses in Europe over those of India. Among the cities steeped in legend and history, Vienna of Europe equals Delhi.

A travelogue will be incomplete without ecstatic reference to the scenes in the Swiss Alps, the pastures and silent valleys in the Himalayas, and the wildlife sanctuaries of the world, some of which are to be found in India, and all the major countries of the world. I was used to our easy ways when one could outrun a slowly accelerating railway train when it just departs from a wayside stop and climb into one's compartment after the train had started. But this would not do in Switzerland. I had stepped out of the train to pick up a coca cola from the station kiosk when the train blew the departure whistle. I finished my drink and then ran to catch the compartment. But the train had locked me out and sped away. I had to find my bag waiting at the next station when I reached it by the next train after an hour. Luckily I had my wife with me who could wait there with the bags. During travels one often meets adventures like the attention of pickpockets, or the presence of an angel of a man or machine. Once I left my briefcase containing my cash and passport on the seat of a bus when getting down at the Toronto railway station. I was advised that the bus will return there in 40 minutes and I might wait there or apply to the lost property office where the bus driver might deposit the unclaimed bag in the evening. I waited there and when the bus returned after about 40 minutes, I picked up my bag from the seat where it had been left by me. One of my friends related to me how his purse containing liquid cash was restored to him by a taxi driver in Delhi where he had left it by mistake. Same was the experience of my wife in Delhi. But I had to cancel my travel when on reaching Calcutta railway station, I discovered that I had lost my purse containing my money and tickets for the short journey I had planned to Santiniketan. Now I take precaution not to carry a billfold and preferably allow my wife to look after the cash and baggage during travel particularly after I lost my briefcase which I left on my seat in the prestigious Rajdhani express at Lucknow just to get a newspaper from the railway platform. When I complained to all and sundry, they all doubted if I had a briefcase since no one dared rob me of it at Lucknow, the cultural hub of the country, in the few minutes I was not holding on to it. The obvious precaution is to carry your briefcase or valuables with you even when going out of train or a plane for a few minutes.

Among capital cities, a disappointing visit was to Cairo. It was impossible to get vegetarian food for my vegetarian wife. She had often to fall back on the perennial bread and potatoes. We enjoyed the visits to the pyramids and the sphinx and the sound and light show. It is amazing to have the ancient Egyptians build the massive pyramids besides hiding considerable knowledge of the stars therein. The taste of the visit was spoiled by their poor hotel keeping. At midnight new allottees seemed to trespass into our room with impunity using the master key from the desk who later profusely apologized for the mistake. I wonder if the hotel industry anywhere can equal this howler.

A visit to London is always exciting. From the devouring of English literature, London and England seem like own country. One naturally wishes to have pilgrimage to the West Minster Abbey, Stratford-on-Avon, the Cambridge and the Oxford universities and many other familiar places from English history and literature. Bernard Shaw, Coleridge, Tennyson, Milton, Sherlock Holmes, Sir Walter Scott, Churchill and so many characters from life or fiction were so real to me. During my stop-over in London while returning from studies in the States, I had good few weeks fully paid holiday in London. A friend who had just returned from profitable purchases of silver in South America purchased a car in London and couple of friends joined him for a grand tour of England. Besides various landmarks mentioned earlier, we visited Stone-henge, Nottingham,

Brighton and other places. My most cherished visit to England was when as a guest of the Royal Society of London on a travel fellowship from the Imperial Relations Trust, I visited well known universities engaged in development studies or in continuing education of engineers. This was in 1980 when we were organizing the open university in Delhi and there was considerable pressure on institutions to assist in the continuing education of scientists and engineers. In order to satisfy the curiosity and my wife's interest in gardens and gardening, they included a visit to the Kew Gardens. We recall with fervour the tea with the director in the Kew Gardens and the many interesting plants he showed us. As a part of this visit we were house guests on a weekend of Sir Stoker who had recently been made the head of his favourite hall at Cambridge. We could also visit Nottingham to again follow the adventures of Robin Hood, but firstly to meet a cousin of mine who is counted among the richest people of Nottingham and who owned one of the two Rolls Royces there.

My twenty-four hours stay at Moscow at the expense of Aeroflot was through a mistake of the commercial staff in Delhi and Helsinki. I was travelling from Helsinki to Delhi via Moscow on a through ticket with prompt connection at Moscow. The airline offices outside Moscow were not aware that in summer the Moscow daylight saving time is one hour ahead of the standard time and so I missed the air connection by about half an hour and they gave me free stay overnight in Moscow. In the hotel I had another interesting encounter. English can help only if you are travelling through the Intourist agency when an interpreter is always around. I stood in a queue apparently for breakfast. When I picked up the items of food and reached the payment counter with my intourist coupon, the girl at the counter calculated the cost of the items and then returned considerable quantity of roubles, since I happened to be in the workers queue while I should have gone to the dining hall where the same food was to be had at much higher cost. I visited the standing exhibition grounds and I am certain, Nehru must have been impressed so that we could have a Pragati Maidan, a permanent venue for trade, etc., exhibitions at Delhi. The Moscow underground is very clean and palatial and it is also the model copied by the Russians when they built the Calcutta underground railway few years later. I had also a leisurely visit to the Kremlin and the Lenin's embalmed remains. It is a strange commentary on human achievement that the edifice of the Soviet state built over so much toil and tears by Lenin and Stalin has gone forever with universal approval, barring the wailing of the true communists of Calcutta and Beijing, and the regret of the Indian state which had developed close and friendly relations with them.

My visit to Budapest was pinched from my scheduled stay at Vienna after the conclusion of the IUGG General Assembly there in 1991. Unfortunately as the train reached there, it started raining and to make the best of my short stay, I could only wander around the fort area and watch the exhibitions in various museums. Just before and after the Vienna visit, I had been to Geneva, Jungfrau, Venice, Frankfurt and Salzburg, the birth place of Mozart. My visits to Brussells, Helsinki, Hamburg, Exeter and Vancouver were in connection with the General Assemblies of the IUGG and IAGA where I was in the habit of discussing my latest results in geophysics. My work has been so much different from the usual, that I had to go again and again to win converts. My prediction to the editor of *Nature* was that I hope to succeed by the year 2002 still few years hence. At Brussells the queen of the Belgians gave a reception in honour of the delegates and believe it or not, she shook hands with each and every one. The Brussells visit is etched in my mind for another reason, while returning *via* Amsterdam to London, I met on the train a girl who happened to ask as to how long I intended staying in Amsterdam. I said I shall be leaving by next available boat. She would not accept this as flattering to her home town. I told her that I happened to have no invitation in Amsterdam. She promptly invited me to stay at her house where her brother's room was vacant and she will like to play the host in Amsterdam. I had wonderful three days there and she showed me all the favourite places of the young students in Amsterdam. We could see the reclaimed land and the reclaiming process, the canals that carry much of traffic, the small island in the harbour well known for its fried eels.

Somehow when I heard about the Soviet occupation of Prague from my Czech hosts, I could imagine the look of surprise on the face of the master when Oliver Twist asked for a second spoon of porridge. The Soviet state was equally surprised when a small state like the Czech Republic claimed to have completed the revolution and swore that it was time for their state to wither away. But this should have happened only in Russia first which was the Big Brother's home state.

Though Washington D.C. cannot boast of centuries of History as the capitals of the old world might do, it has, however, made valiant efforts to be the capital city of the future with possible competitor being Tokyo. Tokyo is much more crowded and Washington has all the space so necessary for a capital of the universal state if it ever came about. New found brotherhood among the white and the black Americans bodes well for the future. I am sure it is not possible to give a complete idea of what scenes and events I have enjoyed in my full life. I have hardly touched my visit to Japan as the guest of the JSPS and perhaps there will be occasion to refer to it later.

After the visit to Vancouver, I went to Boston *via* Davis and San Francisco. At Davis I could enjoy the company for a few days of my cousin Dr. P.N. Vohra now a professor in the Agricultural College of the University of California there. He has been a confirmed bachelor taking particular care to spend his earnings on others. I could see that he was trying to live a life of non-attachment so extolled in Hindu scriptures and succeeding in the relatively congenial environment of a university town. Dr. Vohra has gone out to China, South America and Indonesia as a U.N. or U.S. Aid expert for poultry chemistry or for raising quails, etc. At San Francisco I was the guest of Dr. H.M. Iyer, an Indian geophysicist who has opted to make a career in their Coast and Geodetic Survey. He is an authority on microseisms and interpretation of seismic signals. I could also meet Dr. Umang Gupta, a nephew, a very successful entrepreneur of the Silicon Valley. He has invented a software of use in conversion of management systems and is marketing it through his owned branches in all the important countries of the world. He showed us around the sites of tourist interest in San Francisco, like the market, the harbour, the houses of the rich, the Golden Gate Bridge, etc.

X

IAT and INSA

As stated earlier I became the Director and Dean of the IAT, i.e., Institute of Armament Technology now known as Defence Institute of Advanced Technology at Pune in January 1973, and after retirement (1978) from the Defence Science Service, I was selected as the Executive Secretary of the Indian National Science Academy against a leave vacancy in June 1979. Later in 1981, I was appointed a visiting professor of Physics at Chandigarh for three years.

The Institute at Pune is situated in a most scenic setting. On one side of the Khadagvasla lake is the institute and on the far side is the National Defence Academy with its vast wooded area and pretty buildings. Both the army establishments have a back-drop of hills. The director's bungalow is a palatial house with garages and guest rooms in a large garden of about an acre in area. The garden usually won first prizes in the local flower and garden shows in Pune. The garden is in three terraces below the level of the entrance to the bungalow after a climb along a short winding road from the road skirting the institute. The sunsets over the lake as observed from the garden are most impressive particularly in the rainy season.

The institute was set up to give advanced armament courses to the services officers and to arrange for special technical courses for the newly inducted scientists into the Defence R & D Organization. Due to the exigencies of services, so far the scientist recruits were being given their introduction to ballistics, operational research, elementary armament technologies in short courses or seminars in the Defence Science Centre at Delhi and science orientation courses as well as a technical staff course for the military officers were conducted at the IAT. Only recently a Naval armament course and a Tank technology course had been started and proposals were afoot for a long air armament course. It was also proposed to increase the number per year of the three-month science orientation courses from two to four so that every army officer would undergo that orientation. Due to increase in the sophistication of weapons, there was pressing need for advanced courses as well as introductory courses in guided missiles, air armaments, war gaming, etc. All this required redesigning of the teaching on module basis so that different groups study together the modules of their choice which will be offered in a way that the teacher kept in view the different backgrounds of individual students and their service affiliation. It was to be an exercise in creating the modules and combining these to form different courses. All this was successfully carried out by the staff when I made this the policy for all the courses being offered by the institute. Operational research, management modules and modules on system approach were designed to go along with most courses. I introduced the subject of system approach and used to give few lectures in the appropriate module. A telecommunication course was started and this attracted even students of M.Sc., etc., from other institutions at Pune. Our advanced courses had a compulsory dissertation part which meant that the student had to make almost-original contribution to the teaching of the subject, by mock-ups, by reviewing the numerical data and putting it down in one place, by comparing performance of weapon systems. The institute had advanced research facilities for special subjects, e.g., a wind tunnel, a shock tube, explosion welding, for which an army officer obtained a doctorate from the Bombay IIT. Certain students developed the experimental testing of explosives and rocket fuels, etc., which also led to some physical and chemical research on these subjects and to exchanges with the Explosives Research Establishment. The institute published a journal which had become rather irregular. I corrected this by organizing a regular mailing list by having a life membership in a learned society, viz., Institution of Armament Technologists. Many alumni, staff and students of the IAT as well as officials of the three services and the Ministry of Defence became life members. Using an annual grant from the profits of the canteen we decided to make a nominal payment to authors of review articles accepted for publication. The journal published research notes and other useful articles, book reviews, literature survey, etc., of interest to the armament technologies. The journal is still being regularly published. Symposia were also held and an issue was often devoted to important papers and summary of discussions in the symposium. Each faculty or department was encouraged to have a weekly seminar where the staff or the student officers gave discourses on the dissertation subjects or new developments. I made it a point to attend such weekly seminars. The seminar programme was issued in advance each week so that those interested could plan to attend. The relative isolation of the scientists was overcome by cajoling them to become members of the IAT military mess. The welfare of everyone was sought. The jawans were encouraged to help in the setting up of an IAT dairy farm that assured supply of pure and cheaper milk to every-one. The jawans also were allowed certain vacant hangars for religious worship open to all. I made it a point to inspect the entire estate including the class rooms at least once a month. Beautification of the campus was pursued with vigour. Flower shows were held periodically and prizes were established for the best garden in each category of quarters.

I found that there were not enough playground activities. First of all certain important facilities were added. With the help of heads of the service wings, we added a tennis court, a six-a-side hockey ground, a six hole golf course besides encouraging the faculty to participate in some sport along with the student officers. The Naval wing reorganized the IAT jetty on the Khadagvasla lake as a place for outdoor swimming, boating and sailing.

The institute had its own primary school and after seeing it run successfully for a number of years now the central school at NDA has given it a branch status which assures the children studying in it to get admitted in the central school later. A medical officer and a welfare officer was available. I found the tail comprising the administrative staff was too heavy and replaced some of the staff by more technical officers. The working hours of the institute were increased to full day, i.e., 8 A.M. to 5 P.M. and the working hours of some supporting staff were staggered. The teachers and the taught had thus the facilities for work throughout the day including home work or self-study. The Library and the laboratories were kept open for the full working hours. The students were often given home work to be submitted for evaluation in a week's time. The place became a hive of activity. Many new courses were begun. Some of our officers registered for advanced degrees in the neighbouring institutions. The Institute got recognized as a centre of post-graduate education of the Pune University and I was taken as a member of the University senate as well as their academic council. In 1975, I was elected the chairman of the Pune chapter of the Indian Society for Education and Training.

One job that often came up was to enquire for the Central Government and to submit recommendations for avoiding the losses in the import of costly communication equipment because of inadequate weather protection during the long sea voyage and delay in the clearance of the imported equipment on arrival at the port. Later, government instructions were issued to insist on better than trade packaging as well as to use private clearing agents at the ports.

I noticed that the Maharashtrian industrialists had rather a poor view of Punjabi business partners. They regard them as too ambitious. I made the humorous observation that both in Punjabi as well as in Marathi language pickpockets are known by the same word. The Maharashtrians are given to hymn singing in a group (they sing and dance playing on their hand drums). There is considerable faith in miracles and power of mind over matter with the well known devotees of God (usually Vithal, a name for Krishna). There were stories of miraculous prayer of a family priest of a rich family in a village near Nasik, whose prayer would make an image of his dear god dance and similarly an ordinary photograph of a dead devotee dance in ecstasy in time with the prayer song played on the guitar by the priest. A whole crowd of officer students and staff went in a bus to observe these happenings. We observed these from close quarters. Being not a magician, I was quite convinced of the miraculous performance of the priest. Maharashtra is prone to adding to its pantheon of favourite gods. There have been a large number of saint poets in Maharashtra. Acharya Rajneesh at the height of his popularity set up abode in Pune. After his son, a graduate of IIT Kanpur elected to become a follower of Acharya Rajneesh, my predecessor Brig. Pritampal Singh built a house on the shore of the Khadagvasla lake and settled there after retirement in 1972. I happened to be in USA when the bubble of this saint's popularity burst there. His philosophy is very much a part of Hinduism but is often smothered by the theistic voices. He laid stress on pure life and on freedom from guilt. His more daring followers must have laid stress on freedom from guilt without caring much if the life led was pure or false. His was a gospel of reason and emancipation and will always excite followers towards the evolution of a world view based on human beings and not on human souls or God.

The Chief Controller General, J.R. Samson had taken the initiative to organize a cultural tour for the directors of the Defence Research Organization who could afford from the load of work so that they become more responsive to the needs of the nation. The tour was also to include visits to weapon testing ranges in the country. In the style of the National Defence College, we also visited the famous Jagannath Puri temple. This visit confirmed me in my estimation of worship and miraculous return from worship as practically the impressions of the human mind. The miracle resides in the beholder's mind. At Puri, I happened to be suffering for the past few days from acute eucinophelia causing an involuntary cough every few moments. I felt so incongruous in the company of fellow directors that I took a solemn decision to stake my piety and the holiness of the shrine on the challenge to the divine to cure me right away. Lo, the coughing stopped that instant and I did not have that complaint throughout the remaining tour. Later, on return to Pune, I did take the full course of the medicine as prescribed by the medical officer there. The Hindus have rightly understood the power of prayer. The favour of gods is sought with fervour and the many gods are not miserly about the boons and miracles they scatter. It is immaterial whom and how one worships. As also proven by Shri Ramakrishna, what is required is the intensity of faith and desire to succeed in the person who worships. I had always assumed that miracles must have occurred, but when the wife of my Christian Professor at Lahore mentioned that Christ was the true deity to worship since he was very much alive and manifested himself to the true devotee in dire need, I thought this must be from missionary zeal. But this must also be the matter of faith. I had personally great regard for Guru Nanak. When I thought that my son had not done well in the degree examination and might not pass in the first division, I was sincerely worried. About that time one night I dreamt that Guru Nanak talked to me and reassured me. I am sure if I had been drawn the same way to Christ, I would have seen Christ in that dream. A peculiar feature of my dream was that while I was all the time certain that Guru Nanak was himself speaking to me, but he was a man with black beard and looked possibly around thirty-five years of age. All the pictures of Guru Nanak who lived in the sixteenth century depict him as an older person with white beard. If I were an artist I could now easily draw the picture of the young Guru from my dream.

The IAT was close to Singarh fort, a famous fort in Maratha history. It was the first fort won by frontal attack by Sivaji when he was just collecting his friends to form his conquering army. We often walked up to the high fort. For the purpose of seeing important places nearby, we went to Nasik, Ajanta and Ellora and few times to Bombay. The Karla caves closer to Pune are preserved better than Ellora. The high point about Ajanta is the famous frescos, some of which were in the process of restoration.

The rules had been framed in a fashion that the Defence Scientists could not aspire to rise in service beyond Director Grade I to become say the D.G.R&D. The post of Chief Controller at that time was reserved for a service officer. I had hoped that they will drop this rule within my service tenure, but unfortunately they did so three years after my retirement. One year before retirement I asked for a transfer to Delhi as I had yet to have my house built on a plot acquired there. Since a fellow director had retired there, I was transferred to Delhi as the Director of Scientific Evaluation Group (now called The Institute of System Analysis). This gave me an opportunity to apply my capacity for operational research and system analysis and an opportunity to work closely with groups engaged on management and on research on war gaming and weapon system evaluation. On June 1, 1978, I retired and I did not apply for extension or reemployment, since my own view was that if they could use me further, they should themselves offer a reemployment. But I was told afterwards that they would have perhaps agreed if I had asked for some extension well ahead since as policy in those days, extensions could be given only by the Ministry in exceptional cases and the decision took about a year. During this one year in office at Delhi, I looked into the search theory and gave an alternative method to arrive at the well known results. The new method lends itself beautifully to area searches and my work produced an analytical expression for the probability of success in a search procedure. I could then recommend with confidence the number of aircraft needed for proper search of submarines. We also undertook lectures on management for the three services. A national symposium was convened by me on management. We compared the performance of various weapon systems under appropriate tactics by computer simulation and made recommendations based on system approach.

After retirement I started assisting my friend Shri J.C. Kapur, an industrialist known to me from school days on his solar energy farm near Delhi but soon I gave it up as there came a possibility of appointment as a professor in the Jawaharlal Nehru University where Dr. B.D. Nag Choudhuri who had been the DG R&D few years earlier was the Vice-Chancellor. He first appointed me a member of an Enquiry Committee regarding the working of their branch at Imphal in Manipur State. I visited the Manipur State capital twice. Our recommendations soon led to the independence of this campus as a separate Manipur University. Around this time I was selected as the Executive Secretary of INSA which had the charm that the work would still be at Delhi, and I shall have a chance to look at the government support to scientists mainly channelled through this Academy. In July 1979, I joined INSA at emoluments higher than I would have got on extension within the Defence Science Service. Soon, however, I was disillusioned in the functioning of the Academy because of the cultural imbalance of some of the influential fellows of the Academy. Thanks to the appreciation by Prof. M.G.K. Menon I was offered a visiting professorship of Physics in the Punjab University at Chandigarh for three years, which I readily accepted.

A net loss due to my joining the Indian National Science Academy was that at about that time a proposal to elect me as a Fellow of the Academy matured, but the secretary wrongly advised the chairman of the geophysics committee that an employee of the Academy cannot be elected a fellow. In fact the rules permit the election but debar the fellow to exercise his rights during the period of the employment. The advice was doubly wrong as in any case my employment was limited, being for a leave vacancy. This made me rather indifferent to the fellowship given at the whims of the office holders. Later when a famous past President Prof. D.N. Wadia, FRS informally mentioned to me that he was planning to have me as a fellow in geophysics. I did not desire to reopen the question of conflict with the views of the current Chairman/Secretary and asked him to drop the matter. Prof. Kothari was surprised that I did not take Prof. Wadia at his word since he knew as much of the rules and more about my scientific work than anyone else. Still my stay and work as the Executive Secretary was very rewarding. On the basis of my being the Executive Secretary, I received an invitation to be the guest of the Royal Society of London in their centenary celebrations. The visit was financed by the Imperial Relations Trust of U.K. I have described earlier the programme of the visits. I could also see the working of the scientists of U.K. in the forwarding of science at all levels. They hold special exhibitions giving fully operating key experiments in the development of Physics and Chemistry. The lecture programmes are extensive and meaningful symposia at the borderline of various scientific fields are often organized where the proceedings become landmarks in the development of the subject.

I was also invited by the Japanese Society for the promotion of Science to visit Japan for ten days in order to discuss inter-academy cooperation. They had held some discussions earlier through the Indian Embassy and the CSIR. We filled in actual topics in the approved areas. The Minister of Education was kind enough to spare about half an hour to discuss if Japanese universities could extend to India the type of assistance they give to advanced education in Indonesia and Iran. The subject was later mentioned by me in my report to INSA on return. I must thank both the President of INSA, Prof. M.G.K. Menon and the Japanese authorities who jointly financed my visit and allowed me a full programme of visits to Japanese universities and research establishments being fully aware that on my return to India, I would be relinquishing charge as the executive secretary of INSA to take up my appointment as Visiting Professor in Chandigarh.

The visiting scientists from Japan had evidently given excellent reports about our welcome and arrangements for the visitors especially the lack of any red tape and prompt attention to the requirement of the visitor within the terms of the exchange. I was asked to suggest a suitable programme for my ten days visit. I opted for visits to the high pressure and the seismology sections of the Tokyo University, a visit to their major oceanography institute as well as the museum of mechanized movements likely to help them model insects and organisms for automatic control. I also opted for a visit to Portopia, an island devoted to popularization of science and technology resembling certain parts of Disney World. Along with Dr. Ashoka Jain, the liaison officer from the Indian Embassy, I discussed with the Japanese authorities possible advanced joint symposia under the auspices of the JSPS.

Tokyo reminded me of New York with its overhead trains. The crowds in morning and evening in Tokyo are enormous. The shopping centre Ginza has everything excellently displayed. The government announcements emphasize to the tourist that he must not worry about being overcharged or sold something of quality lower than what he was to expect. They vigorously underlined the honesty of the trader in Japan. One was assured that there was no need at all for a consumer forum in Japan. I am sure if India relearns the value to be placed on one's own word, the efficiency of commerce and business will increase manifold. I wanted to buy a small bag. The shopkeeper fell to talking and when I mentioned that I was the guest of the JSPS, he gave me a hefty discount on his own as a favour to the guest of Japanese Society for the promotion of Science. I also sampled the fast ride in the bullet train to Kyoto from Tokyo on the way to Portopia.

In Japan every effort is made to encourage creativity especially regarding technology in the children. There are competitions and exhibitions of designs by youngsters. The mechanics of movements of sea animals, insects and reptiles are studied, displayed and copied. The Japanese were already leaders in robotics. The Japanese laboratories have glut of equipment and almost any tool required by a researcher is either already available in the vicinity or can easily be fabricated for him.

In July 1981, I took my whole family for a brief holiday visit to Kathmandu in Nepal. When the secretary of the Royal Nepal Academy, learnt about my visit his academy extended full hospitality in Nepal to me and to crown it he accompanied us in visits to the most famous places near Kathmandu. The coexistence and mutual respect of various Indian religions in Nepal is likely to become the norm in secular India since the Hindu ethos whether in India or in Nepal is for religion to confer no special political rights. I experienced also the direct tourist promotion in Nepal which allows some money to all tourists for use in their Casino. Unlike many others we did not lose any of our own money there. A highlight of this visit was the performance of a new version of Kalidas's Shakuntala written by Dr. Ghimre, the President of the Nepal Academy. He has managed the entire play with no intervention of gods but only from the mental turmoil in the main characters.

The INSA is expected to give policy inputs to the government regarding scientific matters. A pre-eminent success was there when the government agreed to protect the Silent Valley from being flooded in Kerala. I had also a humble contribution in this, firstly to reactivate the matter when the proposal made earlier by a lady fellow was in cold storage, and then specially meeting the scientific adviser to the Kerala Government at Trivandrum to gain his support since I had known him from Cornell where both of us were graduate students and in any case most scientists were convinced about environmental conservation.

A major task of the Academy is to recommend Indian scientists for exchange visits to overseas and to provide hospitality to such visitors from abroad. The Academy also gives partial financial assistance to scientists attending symposia and conferences abroad. The Academy publishes a number of journals and annuals. They also select some young scientists for academic awards and in addition awards many medals, awards and emeritus scientist positions to certain outstanding scientists, usually they happen to be fellows of the academy. The style of nominations, selection committees and the final approval of the council is dutifully followed, but mostly the nominations went through only if one member of the selection committees happened to pursue it energetically or if one had the support of someone at about the apex of scientific management in India.

The Academy encouraged popular lecturers, symposia and conferences, but the standard seen in BBC or even on Indian TV now was not yet reached at that time. I had gone privately to U.S.A. where I was happy to receive an invitation from the AAAS to visit them in Washington since they wanted to discuss the modality of a prestigious inter-academy symposium in New Delhi on the role of non-governmental organizations and the national and international scientific societies in the development efforts. The symposium was a great success later. I had also been instrumental in organizing a joint symposium in New Delhi with the Disaster Institute of U.K. on the management of calamities. The then Foreign Secretary of the Royal Society had mooted the idea and the symposium was also attended by Roger Revelle among others. I understood later that Roger Revelle's comments were not liked by some in India.

I suppose no serious effort is ever wasted. I had kept learning foreign languages and retained some reading knowledge of Spanish, French, Russsian and German. This knowledge assisted me in speedy disposal of correspondence from foreign academies and associations. Many foreign scientists brought with them token gifts for the Academy and sometimes for me in person. We also were liberal with our time. I often received them and saw them off at the airport. (Now they have created a separate post in the academy for these tasks). When the visiting dignitary came accompanied, my wife invariably helped them see local sights in Delhi and visit the Cottage Industries Emporium.

A big event was the total solar eclipse in 1981 visible in Hyderabad where most scientists trying various experiments at the time of the solar eclipse, had concentrated. I camped there for a few days for seeing that the Academy's assistance was reaching the scientists sponsored by us. The sight of the total eclipse was unforgettable. The Academy journal printed a beautiful picture of the solar eclipse on its front page.

As the executive secretary I was often required to travel to various science centres in the country since the academy holds council meetings each quarter at usually different places from where there might have been an invitation. Executive secretary with skeleton staff also has to be there couple of days in advance so that the council meeting proceeds without any hitch and there is a full programme to keep the scientists busy. During my tenure I attended council meetings at Delhi, Calcutta, Goa, Srinagar, Hyderabad, Udaipur, etc. This gave me an opportunity to renew my friendships with the scientists and others at these places.

While working as the executive secretary I also completed my manuscript on "Materials and Environment" which was duly published in 1982 by Interprint of Delhi. The Foreign Secretary and Director N.P.L., Dr. A.R. Verma was the convener of INSA symposium on management in which I took considerable interest beyond the routine one of an executive secretary. Some special tips for R&D managers concern the creation and maintenance of the creative environment. The creative workers have to be shielded from bureaucratic buffets unlike some managers who count on these to suppress the good workers to grind some paltry axe or simply not to offend the aggressive bureaucrats. The publication policy should be carefully enunciated and followed. Various management routines should be reduced to time bound automatic steps for increase of well-being and efficiency. An R&D manager must at all times be attentive to incentives and advanced seminars. The workload should be continuously given or checked so that there is neither idle equipment nor is the supervising ability of the senior people lying unused. One must guard against the growth of a large administrative tail. The travel funds for scientists should not be lacking. A motivated scientist is a real asset.

On 1st July, 1981, I joined the University of Punjab as a visiting Professor of Physics.

XI

Visiting Professor and After

The move to Chandigarh as visiting professor (When I earned Eminent Scientist Award) was very beneficial financially to me and changed my whole future. There I was assured of accommodation for three years and so I rented out my beautiful house at Vasant Vihar in New Delhi. I discovered that the rents were very high and the situation was very popular with foreigners on tenure employment at Delhi. Even after the job in Chandigarh, I could now count on steady income for life from renting out this house which I did on permanently shifting to Vasant Kunj in 1989 to a flat placed at my disposal by my daughter living in the States. This is how I could continue to carry out my research and writing at home since then.

The chairman of the Physics Department Prof. V.M. Bhanot when I reported to him informed me that as visiting Professor, I had no duties in the department. My appointment was made for my considerable expertise in geophysics which unfortunately was not taught in the department but if I was ready, they would start a special paper in geophysics for the M.Phil. students, and for the present I could do what I liked and be available for some assistance to the department if required. This suited me and at start I brushed up my knowledge of solid state physics and in the very beginning I found lot of confusion and unfinished business around the activity coefficients. Soon I could write a new theory which was published in the Proceedings of the INSA. There has to be an interpretation of atomic orbits leading to alteration in valency. In the meanwhile Shri Tarlok Singh of the Indian Council of World Affairs (on the suggestion from the department of Ocean Technology) asked me if I was agreeable to write a study on Oceanographic advances in India for consideration of a UNDP seminar on regional cooperation for the development of Marine resources in the South Asia region. A paper was to be presented in 1983 at Male in the Maldives in a workshop arranged by the Marga Institute of Colombo. I was allotted a reasonable budget for the study and I could visit in this connection the oceanography and fisheries institutions in India and responsible Ministries in Delhi for the thorough preparation of the study. The study was completed in time and copies were distributed internationally by the Indian Council of World Affairs. Later I published it after certain additions as a book "Development of Marine Resources—India" by Concept, Delhi, 1988. I had gone to Male *via* Colombo in 1983. Soon afterwards the ethnic strife flared up to an insurgency and communal rioting in Sri Lanka and my sympathies were naturally with all the sufferers but more so with the staff and scholars of the Marga Institute.

Maldives, a holiday resort particularly popular with German speaking tourists, can also be a tourist haven for Indians who in any case often go to Sri Lanka or Mauritius. A joint deep sea fishing fleet for SAARC countries could operate from Maldives. Maldives has whole islands marked for various functions, like a five star hotel, an airport, an oil depot, etc., etc. The city of Male has no metalled roads. The shallow sea upto the coral reef is tourists' paradise for sea diving and exploration. The people live by fishing or as sailors on ships of many lands. The President of the Maldives held a dinner reception for the participants of the workshop at their island hotel and one could sample the pan-Indian cuisine at its best which is now the craze of the west. I was shocked to hear few years later that even the placid waters of the lagoons around Maldives could be disturbed by a pirate coup from across the sea and was glad that the Government of India took speedy action on the request from the President of the Republic of Maldives and rescued the Government from being hijacked by a mafia type operation. Already pirate dens are operating from certain spots near Singapore and in the South China Sea in the eastern hemisphere. Active regional cooperative organizations will be the guarantee for safe shipping in these areas.

It was indeed a pleasure to prepare a course to cover essentials of geophysics including oceanography and meteorology in about forty lectures for post-graduate science students who generally had no initial knowledge of geology or astronomy. Each lecture for them was almost covering practically a whole book. Because of the highly compressed and encapsulated knowledge in each lecture there was soon a protest. I accordingly promised to prepare with the help of notes of certain students of my lectures, a detailed set of notes, which was done well ahead of the examination and a copy was distributed to all the students. These notes led to my writing a comprehensive book on "Introduction to Geophysics: of the Solid Earth, the Oceans and the Atmosphere", which is now being updated. The University Grants Commission had a scheme where certain established departments in universities were identified for further financial assistance to become Centres for Advanced Studies in respective areas. Punjab University got such centres in Botany and later in Geology. Thus there was considerable activity in the sciences with the cyclotron already operational in the Physics department and a special centre for instrumentation having been sanctioned by the government for the entire State in the Punjab University. I gave some extension lectures on cloud physics in the department in addition to a set of invited University lectures on the formation of the earth. Course work at M.Phil. level within the Ph.D. term of post-graduate students is quite appropriate for India since we do not have rather advanced courses at M.Sc. level while in U.K. such courses involving great amount of work for both the teachers and the taught are given at B.Sc. level. The students then proceed to the thesis work purely by self-study and research. In U.S.A. there is considerable advanced course work in the first year after induction into Ph.D. programme. I understand, many universities including the Punjab University have given up the condition that Ph.D. candidates must first complete the requirements for the M.Phil. degree mainly by course work. The teaching of Geophysics was, therefore, discontinued after I left Punjab University in 1984.

There were strong groups working on thin films and particle physics, and I had first intended to pick up some research problem in these areas but while teaching geophysics I found that the structures of the earth had been based on the old work of Birch and Jeffreys and had not been rechecked or progressed further. The ideas about the absence of uranium in the core of the earth did not appeal to me. Soon enough when I expressed my doubts, Dr. H.M. Iyer pointed out a newly published paper stating that uranium was in solution in molten iron. I started working out the structure of the earth *ab initio* from the tabulated data of contents of atoms in solar system and in meteorites and the known ratio of silicon and iron in the earth. I published my findings in a paper on the "Innermost Core of the Earth" in the Proceedings of INSA. I had seen no reason not to have excess copper from what could be held in solution in the iron core, to appear as a melt closer to the centre of the earth. I also wondered why heavy elements like uranium, thorium. Hafnium, etc., though in proportionally very small amounts would not gravitate in the thousands of years to the centre of the earth to form an innermost core. I pursued this effort to the logical conclusion that there would be shells of the uranium and thorium on the outside of the innermost solid core which itself will be isolated from the solid iron core by a fused mass of copper or copper-iron alloy. Further gravitational separation might produce a thin layer of ^{235}U which would grow to critical thickness to give a spontaneous explosion abetted by the presence of huge mass of uranium and thorium of the neighbouring shells. Such an explosion could be strong enough to provide the power to eject a piece of earth's crust as a scab to form the core of the moon around which other dust material will accumulate to build up the moon. Such an hypothesis had been considered by other scientists too but they dropped it because they could not imagine the force which could drive out the scab to a distance beyond the Roche limit. My hypothesis could also give answer to many unsolved problems. The fission explosion would also be the source of copious production of helium. Helium is still given out by the earth and according to the information gleaned from the Soviet scientists, Dr. S.D. Chatterji of Calcutta had inferred that 100,000 litre equivalent at N.T.P. was the emission of helium per day from the earth. I gave a radio talk on this subject in 1983 through the courtesy of the Director General of All India Radio, M.S. Batra and later in two invited lectures in the Birla Science and Technology Museum at Calcutta. I developed a theory of the origin of terrestrial magnetism from the ferromagnetism of helium amplified by the paramagnetism of the iron core. Such ideas led to the origin of various planetary magnetic fields explaining their direction as well.

Papers were presented at successive IUGG meetings. Simple physical considerations led me to calculate the temperature of the innermost core as 6858 K. The planetary axial tilts and the origin of satellites could all be included in a single theory. There are not yet many converts to these ideas because the earth scientists are not yet prepared to imagine the occurrence of atomic explosions in the earth of long ago although I have lined up irrefutable evidence for this in my paper on Atomic explosions published in the Proceedings of INSA. At the moment many scientists invoke collisions of arrivals from outside the solar system with planets to produce satellites and rings, while my views do not require such visitors from outer space.

Teachers in the Punjab University as well as in other universities are organized like a trade union and so are the students. This interferes with any improvements that the University Grants Commission might suggest to the Universities. This is a legacy from the colonial days and our inadequate view of democracy or socialism. Trade unionism in educational institutions is incongruous, to say the least. When the University Grants Commission authorized certain funds to each university for appointment of one or more Visiting Professors, the teachers union of Chandigarh agitated for the merger of such funds with the funds allotted to the head "staff" in the university so that regular teachers could get more promotions!

The university campus is very pretty. The petunias planted around roadside trees look enchanting. The Botanical garden of the university provided an excellent place for our morning walk. Unfortunately in a subsequent visit to Chandigarh I found some officious department head has debarred morning walks of staff or students there, pretending that such few addicts harm the tranquillity of the plants and compel the garden staff to be on their toes too long. The science attache of the French Embassy at Delhi once spent a couple of nights at Chandigarh. He asked me if I could recommend any night life at Chandigarh. I had to explain it to him that apart from metropolitan cities, Indian towns and villages have only morning life and no night life. Everybody chirps and hymns in the morning. There are innumerable temples, gurudwaras and mazars at it. At dusk people retire to within the family.

In 1982, when I got a regular university quarter, my next door neighbour was a "Sikh intellectual" who used to regularly attend the gatherings in the hills of the Sikh students organization. Some Pakistani Muslims came to reside with him since he had made friends in Pakistan when each year he would go there as a Sikh pilgrim. He praised their hospitality and friendship. He had been one of the framers of the Punjabi dictionary and helped them to translate BHAGOTI of the Sikh prayer with the meaning sword, while truly it was the name of the mother goddess of the ancient Punjabi faith so dear to Guru Govind Singh. This crude deception was made in the interest of cutting the Sikh faith from its true Hindu moorings. This teacher became the head of the university Punjabi department after the killing of Dr. Tewari at the hands of the terrorists. This was the time when Bhindranwala was alive and spreading his hate Hindu and hate India gospel; see also *Conflicts and Coexistence* by J.N. Nanda, Concept, 1992.

The first target of the fanatics or the fundamentalists among the Sikhs were the Nirankaris, among whom were both Hindus and Sikhs. Their fault was that they tried to spread their sect right in Amritsar, the sacred city of the Sikhs. This was the type of liberty for others in their mind that day, on the other hand Guru Nanak freely criticized Hindu worship in the sacred cities of Hardwar and Jagannath Puri in the sixteenth century with impunity and rather approval of so many among the Hindus. By the time I left Chandigarh in 1984, operation Blue Star had already taken place and Mrs. Gandhi was later shot in 1986. When I happened to visit Chandigarh in 1985 or 1987, there was a big change; it presented a scene of a beleaguered city. Though the people avoided any local Hindu-Sikh communal clash, yet they were frightened out of their wits. The roads were blocked every couple of kilometres by the police. The militants ruled the streets and roads from sunset to sunrise. The village priests and gurudwaras took the line laid down by the militants. Many innocent bus passengers, professionals, and labourers were mercilessly cut down by the militants who killed more nationalist Sikhs than others. The burden of murderous attacks on newspaper hawkers and media men particularly of the *Hind Samachar* group was enormous. My nephew in Jalandhar had shown respect to a fallen victim of the terrorists. He was marked for punishment and shot while working in his office. By 1992, the tide began to turn in the Punjab. The Pakistani support was more needed in J&K for the contrived revolt of the Muslims there, inspite of the democratic rights and autonomy they enjoyed under the Indian humane laws. Only now are people realizing the true ambition of Pakistan of attempts to ruin India than help the people of the Indian States like Punjab, J&K, etc. After all it had already lost Bangladesh due to its repressive policies and worse was happening in their Sindh and Baluchistan provinces.

With Chandigarh as base I had an opportunity to travel to various interesting places in the Punjab especially since it would be an occasion for my grown up sons to sample the life of the Punjab to which they had been alien even when they spoke Punjabi. First we visited Phagwara where my mother's folks had their roots. Being Bedis they were a mixed Hindu-Sikh family. They owned and maintained a gurudwara there up to recent times until all the direct descendents of my maternal grandfather moved out of Phagwara, and a different branch of the family now controls the gurudwara. My cousin Lt. Col. (Retd.) C.B. Bedi now lives at Chandigarh where he does some honorary work for the Bhartiya Vidya Bhavan there. He has studied deeply the history of his family and of the Sikhs in general including the inside wrangling of the Akali leadership that led by default to the extremism of Bhindranwala. In his company we visited the gurudwaras in Anandpur, Sirhind, and monuments in Basi. Basi Pathana is a place of pilgrimage for the Afghans (Pathans) since many Pathan holy men made it their own. In the week-end outings of the teachers groups we visited the famous temples of the mother goddess like Naina Devi and Chandi, etc. We also visited the Nangal Dam, the Roper canal system and the Bhakra Dam.

My younger son after his internship at Chandigarh had joined the M.S. studies in surgery at the Christian Medical College at Ludhiana. Ludhiana is the most industrialized city in the Punjab where almost every house is a factory. They have built a spacious and beautiful all inclusive temple dedicated to many gods. There is a replica also of the famous Vaishno Devi shrine in it and those who may not undertake the arduous pilgrimage in Jammu region can have the benefit from visiting the replica here. The Punjab Agricultural University is also situated there. Dr. Sukhdev Singh happened to be the Vice-Chancellor there whom I knew from Delhi. He had asked me over in some staff selection committee work and was kind enough to show the great strides the university had made in pushing forward the green revolution in the Punjab. We also visited Kurukshetra, one of the holiest spots for Hinduism where Shri Krishna taught the *Gita* to Arjuna in the *Mahabharata* war. I was struck with the excellent arrangements for the tourists and pilgrims that exist there. Within the department, I became rather friendly with Prof. S.P. Puri who was writing under U.G.C. auspices textbooks on various topics of physics. His wife later became the dean of medical sciences in the university. It was in his company that I visited the famous god-man Dadaji who was reported to be capable of minor miracles, but I found the statements rather exaggerated as is customary when such men are seeking disciples and followers and he seemed to be doing a professional job of it in cohorts with learned friends in the university. His favourite miracle was touching someone perfunctorily and making him reek with some kind of an aroma for at least few hours. His disciples demonstrated his ability to guide them into a trance. This much need not be any deception as this is what the seekers throng to them for.

On the expiry of the term as Visiting Professor, since my house at Delhi was still occupied by tenants, I planned to move to Dehradun where my son Dinesh was posted at ONGC headquarters. He was yet unmarried and we wanted to keep house for him till he could marry a suitable girl. About this time I got an invitation from the organizers of the triennial conferences on the unity of sciences to attend their International Conference in Washington D.C. at their expense and particularly to take part in the symposium on Oceans and Man. The entire expense of travel and hospitality in Washington was to be borne by them. They also allowed my wife to accompany me. I planned the visit in a way that I could spend few weeks with my daughter at Dover (Mass) during the return journey from Washington D.C. The conference was highly enlightening to me. There were learned papers on philosophy that impels people to be creative in science of all kinds. The members discussed the progress of scientific and social science paradigms in various stages. In the oceanography sessions, the main problem under discussion became the timing of the appearance of the oceans on the earth, a problem that had close link with the appearance of the moon. Prof. R.A. Lyttleton FRS worked up an interesting theory about the early history of the earth-moon system. He was clear that earth was formed solid and became a liquid mass later due to energy from radioactive disintegrations. He also felt that the earth has been contracting and the release of water happened due to some upheaval like the episodic formation of the moon by the pull of a visiting star. Prof. Fred Singer posed the problem that it would be important to settle once for all whether the earth was formed solid or liquid. As stated earlier I was already working on the internal structure problem and after this conference I worked harder on these issues leading to string of results mentioned briefly earlier. During my stay at Dover, I approached the Department of Dynamic Oceanography of Harvard University for some facility for my theoretical researches. Prof. A.R. Robinson, the head of the department allowed me a guest status in the department without any further ado or formality. He gave me an office and a key to the department library and I revised my calculations about the structure of the earth and the flooding by vortex trailing behind a cyclonic storm while there. I was also given staff membership of the Harvard University Library. This was a great contrast to Indian institutions who hardly recognize a retired scientist as fit for work. My name was suggested by the Director N.I.O. for attachment as a specialist to the Institute of Oceanography at Goa, but they refused since I was soon approaching sixty-five years of age!

I returned to Delhi on the day Mrs. Gandhi was shot by her security guard. After attending IUGG meeting at Hyderabad where I was invited by the convener to speak about the radioactive heat from the innermost core, I went to a retired life at Dehradun. I began writing two books there, one on the subject of India's transformation in the twentieth century which was published in 1986 under the title *Science and Technology in India's Transformation* by Concept, Delhi. Shri M.S. Batra who had retired from his post as DG of the All India Radio was so carried away with the contents that at his recommendation, the President of India, Giani Zail Singh was pleased to release it from the Rashtrapati Bhavan, in a glittering ceremony attended by many important people of Delhi. I believe the book found its way to the shelves of many libraries in India and abroad. The institutions like the National Defence College and many staff colleges made it recommended reading. The other book I started writing was on geophysics and I could do this only because I could use the libraries of the Himalayan Geological Institute and the ONGC. I hope the manuscript will be published, but the publishing of the scientific books takes time in India. The delay has already necessitated a thorough revision.

Dehradun is a lovely town reached by a winding road from Saharanpur. It is the base for going to the hill station of Mussoorie. In summer the whole resort of Mussoorie is a fair ground and fiesta town. Few years earlier I had gone with my family to spend a summer there. Dehradun is only about 30 km from the holy city of Haridwar on the Ganges. It is a pleasing scene to witness the evening worship of the Ganga when earthen lamps and flower petals are floated downstream by the worshippers along with the accompaniment of songs, conch shells and bells. We had also an occasion to visit Haridwar on the Kumbh Fair when about a million people had assembled there for the holy dip or to renew their faith by mixing with the multitude of the faithful. Luckily we returned to Dehradun one day before the stampede that cost many lives. I also went few times by road from Dehradun to Chandigarh. The road goes along the top of the wooded hills passing the city of Nahan and a geology park where fossil trees of bye-gone ages are to be seen. On the way close to Dehradun is also Paonta Sahib, a well frequented gurudwara. It is a place of historical interest. The rock edict of Ashok at Kalsi is well preserved. We also visited the Renuka Lake, a place of pilgrimage and a scenic spot.

From Dehradun we came to live in Delhi almost permanently first in own house when it was vacated by the tenants and later in the flat purchased by our daughter in Vasant Kunj. In 1987 and 1989, I presented my results about the origin of the planetary magnetism at IUGG and IAGA General Assemblies at Vancouver and Exeter (UK) respectively. I wrote the book on *Conflicts and Coexistence* published later by Concept at Delhi in 1991 and a manuscript on *Secularism and Social Justice* still knocking at the doors of publishers, using my copious reading in the Harvard University Library, the library of the United Services Institute, and the library of the Jawaharlal Nehru University at Delhi. By trudging with a candidate in the bylanes and on village paths in a backward district of the U.P. during his election campaign in 1991, I had an interesting experience about Parliamentary Elections in India. The candidates spend money and exert hard. The public has yet to be educated to choose with eyes open, and to concentrate on the ideology of the political parties and the personal merits and values of the candidate that deserve their votes. I wish all success to the valiant efforts being made toward election reform and to instil accountability into the minds and practices of the politicians as well as the media.

Last year or so, I spent in writing these memories of my life and activities. I am now a looking forward to, fresh start in the promotion of democratic secular life and multi-religious persons in India. I have begun taking interest in a new organization: "Secular Life Society of India". This is for the global effort for underscoring new values for one united world.

That is why I emphasize in this humble effort the New Mahayana for the world where people have to rediscover virtue suitable for the life together of diverse races, regions, and philosophies. People must learn to ventilate their differences and come together in reason without coming to blows. We have learnt that at the time of the Buddha and for few centuries around it, public discussions of different propositions were carried out in the presence of judges and the public agreement was found on the most appropriate wisdom.

XII

Dehradun and Back to Delhi

My term as a Visiting Professor expired in 1984. After attending an international symposium abroad, I returned to Delhi in 1986 and decided to make a fresh career there as a guest worker in the Jawaharlal Nehru University School of Environmental Sciences with the courtesy of the then head Prof. Keshavan. As a memory of his kindness I still use the special membership of the JNU library which he got approved for me. I made a good friend in the Deputy Librarian who had the plan to start a publishing business to be carried forward after his retirement by his son Ashish Verma. It was with the great help given by him in preparing my manuscript of the comprehensive book on Geophysics that I got as the first publication of his enterprise in 1997. A second publication was on *Foreign Policy of Co-existence—India*. The period 1984-1986 was spent with my son who had entered as a scientist with newly set up Oil and Natural Gas Commission at Dehradun. Using the facilities offered by the Himalayan Institute of Geology there, I wrote the first draft of my book on geophysics. The highlight of this period was the selection of my son as a participant in the first Oceanography cruise to the Antarctica. On the cruise itself he became friendly with a girl participant (Gowrie) and on return they got engaged when I was at Dehradun and the marriage was celebrated when my wife and I returned to Delhi to reoccupy our house that was vacated in 1986 as per agreement by the tenants. In order to augment my income from the pension from my service in Defence Research Organization, I decided to move to a flat under construction for my daughter in Vasant Kunj while she had to continue to stay at Dover, a suburb of Boston in USA where her husband was starting on a lucrative medical career. This became a permanent financial solution for me since my own house in Delhi was to bring in high rent which was doubled when I added a second floor to it later.

My younger son who had as a matriculate spurned the almost sure selection as Central Government scholar for a career in agricultural research giving his preference for medical profession in surgery as the reason. He had plodded on to become a surgeon securing the M.S. qualifcation from the prestigious Christian Medical College at Ludhiana. His marriage was arranged in the new fashion (self-arranged with support of both sets of parents) in 1991. He and his wife, a daughter of a working general in the Medical Service of the army, were not satisfied with prevailing jobs for physicians available with the Government Health Scheme and prepared for migrating to USA and again he had to plod for considerable time to secure a surgeon's job in the USA. He lives now in a palatial house in the beautiful state of West Virginia and they are raising a family there as US citizens. The wife is a successful school teacher and the daughter is top of her school class. They have younger son who unfortunately suffers from diabetes Class I, and they are waiting advances in stem-cell research to cure it.

Dehradun is a beautiful town on the foothills of the higher peaks crowned with the resort town of Mussoorie. In summer most gentry of northern plains flock to resort towns in the hills. Mussoorie is most popular with the city folks of the Punjab, Haryana and Delhi. The city is practically a market for local products and city produce for the hill folk. It has a scenic circular waterfall about 100 metres high where the upper level rain water drops to the level of Dehradun and then flows away with small temples built on the banks of the flowing stream. Dehradun has the well known Indian Forest Research Institute with considerable teaching programme and many students from abroad also study there. The Research Institute's museum is worth a visit. The city is surrounded by tea gardens and gardens of *lichi* fruit.

The *lichi* fruit has a short span in which the fruit has to be removed from the tree, packed with lot of tree leaves and then sent to capital city markets.

The climate was particularly attractive for development and manufacture of optical and photographic goods. There are a number of research establishments around Dehradun particularly set up by the Council of Scientific and Industrial Research and Instrument Development Laboratories for the Defence.

The pious folk visit Haridwar a pilgrim's town on the Ganges which is close to Dehradun and many convenient trains in the plains for Haridwar connect to Dehradun. The Indian penicillin factory is also on the way. The road from Delhi to Dehradun touches the Corbett National Park popular with visitors longing to have a look at the Indian wild fauna. The through trains between Kolkata and Amritsar/Chandigarh do not pass through Dehradun requiring train transfer at the rail junction. Lashkar.

During my stay at Dehradun, since Dinesh often travelled between Delhi and Dehradun, I also traversed this road many times and enjoyed road side refreshment in the middle at the well developed Deer Park by private entrepreneurs.

The highlight of our stay in Dehradun was the visit of Gowrie and her mother when they wanted to assess the family and religious outlook of the family where Gowrie had chosen her future to lie. The approval was indicated by all sharing the sweets brought in by the Gowrie's mother. Dinesh and Gowrie had been both participants on the first Indian oceanography cruise to the Antarctica and had decided to marry subject to Gowrie obtaining the approval of her modernized parents who in fact believed in children making own choice. Later when I had moved to Delhi, the marriage was celebrated in 1986 according to South Indian Brahmanical rites which are not much different from Khatri marriages in the Punjab who believe themselves to be true representatives of ancient Hindus of India, a belief very much foreign to the views of South Indian Hindus who regarded Punjabi Hindus to be too much influenced by Islam and the anti-idolatrous inclination of the Arya Samaj which dominated the Punjab scene or from devotion to the Sikh Gurus for the last few centuries who were also against Hindu worship at various sacred places. In 1986, we had moved back to Delhi from Dehradun when the tenant vacated our house at Delhi according to the agreement.

When my house at Delhi was vacated, I picked up new life there. I started working as guest scientist at Jawaharlal Nehru University School of Environmental Sciences and completed my book on Geophysics. I started on a new career of writing books on pressing problems faced by India. I began talking about secularism being of prime importance with equal regard for all religions.

In 1989, my younger son, Rajesh got engaged to Lt. General (Dr.) J.K. Khurana's daughter Benu, It was so subtly arranged marriage that both Rajesh and Benu who had always stood for freedom of choice, thought of the arranged marriage as self-arranged love marriage. In 1991 Rajesh went on an employee visa to USA in search of a surgery career there. After considerable struggle he got a good emergency doctor's appointment in the regional hospital at Daniels (West Virginia) in USA. Benu had an appointment earlier in USA as a qualified teacher and has been teaching Chemistry to high school pupils. They have prospered there and are now US citizens. West Virginia is very much scenic and comes close to Himachal in greenery and flowing streams. An interesting monument to see in West Virginia is the underground capital dug under the hills for occupation in an emergency of say a nuclear war. The underground capital complex is now maintained as a museum but in ready for occupation status. Rajesh lives in a palatial home at a resort area of lake drive in West Virginia. Unfortunately their son Tanuj a gifted sportsman and an obedient son has suffered since childhood from Type I incurable diabetes. He can give daily injection of medicine himself and is courageously living a normal school boy life in the school where Benu is a teacher. Rajesh's daughter was honoured by her school when she passed out to join on a state scholarship the West Virginia University.

In 2010 on the retirement from governorship, my friend Dr. A.R. Kidwai wishing to rejuvenate Zaheer Science. Foundation came to live in Delhi and start his science policy interest as Chairman of the Zaheer Science Foundation (ZSF). The ZSF has own building partly still under construction at Delhi. I have been asked to function as the Director of ZSF with him as Chairman. Dr. Kidwai found merit in my geophysical research. I have sent papers for publication which make up my new theory of Earth's Interior and the Origin of the Moon as well as the earth's magnetism. The ZSF is interested in the efforts nationwide to speedily spread capability in basic sciences in India.

XIII

Scientific Contribution and Published Books

I. Oceanography

1. I was the member of the Geophysics Sub-committee of the International Indian Ocean Expedition 1961-1964 when the Physiography diagram of the Indian Ocean was published by Bruce C. Heezen and Marie Tharp of the Columbia University. Pakistan diplomacy held it as an endorsement of their view of the Rann of Kutch being part of the open ocean. I had to answer the charge from India that there was no such indication. The choice of the sketch was entirely normal for those days since new sketches were not available to the authors in USA and the depth soundings in coastal regions up to ten miles of the coast line were not included in the diagram for the Indian Ocean.

2. On the invitation of the Scripps Institute of Oceanography, I participated in the leg from Callao (Peru) to Easter Island and then to San Diego, of their Downwind Expedition. I carried out my experiment to verify my method of instantaneous estimation of fish catch below the fishing vessel in the open ocean. It was confirmed that when my method predicted poor fishing there, the actual fishing was negligible. For fishing a vast area of the ocean from Easter Island to the equator is barren of biological content. Actual attempt at line fishing at many spots on the passage confirmed this. The experiment was published in scientific journal (*American J. of Acoustics*) in 1978.

The international fisheries research has not caught on to this convenient method since it needs a separate modified echo sounder equipment for monitoring the biological content under the vessel in the entire sea water column. My research was in response to the recommendation of the Commonwealth Conference on Oceanography (1954), at the National Institute of Oceanography in U.K. which I had attended as sole delegate from India, desiring a facility to monitor instantaneously the production in the ocean,

3. I set up the Indian Naval Physical Laboratory at Cochin in 1953 which has now grown into the prestigious Naval Physical and Oceanography Laboratory at Thevra (Ernakulam) with a Naval ship at its disposal for scientific work. The ship had also participated in the International Indian Ocean Expedition when I measured the depth of sea bottom under the mud off Cochin harbour by seismological experiment. Along with Prof. E.C. La Fond, the American scientist regarded as the father of physical oceanographic studies at Waltair, I promoted such studies at Cochin and Waltair and also had La Fond as a life long friend. As Member-Secretary of the Indian National Oceanography Committee, I was active in the setting up of the National Institute of Oceanography at Goa which had Dr. S.Z. Kasim as its first Director and also the initiator of Indian Research Station on Antarctica.

4. Naval Research was started by me at Cochin as deputy to the British adviser on Naval research, Dr. G.E. Gale, invited to work with Dr. D.S. Kothari, the Scientific Adviser to Raksha Mantri and work on underwater sound and on microseisms was begun there. Measurement of parameters like temperature and salinity and ocean currents was routinely begun. BT observations were routinely tabulated from data gathered by surface vessels. Papers on origin of microseisms published in the Journal of Geophysical Research have become resource papers. An interesting observation was that from floating card experiment for understanding ocean currents off the west coast of India, a card reached and was picked up off the west coast of Australia. It possibly must have hugged the northern coast of Java before going across the ocean to Australia.

II. Internal Structure of the Earth

1. My most important work so far has been on the internal structure

of the earth and the moon and the subject of earth science will be different from what exists in current textbooks. I have already mentioned in the chapter on life at Washington D.C. how I started work on earth Physics as a step to understand the origin of long period microseisms not assignable to storm causes. About five billion years ago, the uranium content of meteorites was fairly large. The earth grew in size as a liquid sphere on account of high energy release when the meteorite came to a stop on the surface of the growing earth; one can see the evidence from the splashes on the fall of the meteorite on the moon. In the growing fluid earth there was considerable amount of atomic iron that assisted in the break up of oxides and chemical compounds, the elements would be in atomic state and by gravity differentiation, elements heavier than iron will accumulate as solids when the melting point was higher than that of iron at the centre of the earth. This constitutes the innermost core and from the data regarding composition of the meteorites, the size of the innermost core is determined to be a sphere of 33 km radius. Uranium will form a sphere of radius 13.4 km. With time even the isotope ^{235}U will separate from bulk uranium and form a thin layer on the outer surface of the uranium sphere. When this layer increases to a critical thickness an atomic fission explosion will occur. We imagine that every planet would be likely to have an atomic explosion in its early evolution. The copper of the meteorites will accumulate in a liquid shell from radius 33 km to 150 km and next will be the iron shell reaching to its outer radius 1216 km as determined by the seismologists. The existence of this copper shell is confirmed by the larger radial velocity of the P waves wrongly being assigned to crystalline structure of solid iron in deep core conditions.

2. Next important result is the identification of the origin of earth's magnetism is induced magnetism of solidified iron in the earth; the induction was from the field of the self-aligned nuclear magnetic moments of the ^{3}He atoms produced by the atomic explosion in addition to the very small 5nT cosmic magnetic field of space. The occurrence of another isotope of helium in much larger quantity is responsible for longer stability of the inducing field and the interplay of the two isotopes of helium can explain the observed magnetic reversals and the aborted reversals. The dynamo theory is stretched to have the convection currents in spite of absence of required

viscosity and by overlooking the observed stabilized liquid layering in the fluid core. The calculations based on the existence of the inducing field and the possibility of iron under core conditions being paramagnetic give the observed magnetic field outside and close to the earth.

The Dynamo Theory has been the work horse of earth scientists. So many dynamos were discussed bringing forth magnetic fields in sundry situations. Apart from the often published comments about lack of required viscosity in the fluid necessary for convection currents in the actual earth, the observed layer structure in the fluid core of the earth militates against the dynamo origin of the main magnetic field of the earth. Kent C. Condie has also concluded in his book published in 2005 that a dynamo will not fit the requirements of earth's magnetism.

3. I have been able to solve the riddle of tilting of planets. The scientists seem to regard the tilt of planets (the axis of rotation being at an angle to the axis of revolution of the planet) as a whim of nature and what happens as a fact of creation. This is not actually so. The obvious cause is the atomic explosion that causes some mass to be expelled out of the planet. Such an expulsion from a rotating planet can cause a tilting of the axis of rotation when the moment of inertia of the planet can hardly be affected. From the observed tilt the amount of mass expelled can be calculated. The expelled mass is the starting point of a new pro-grade satellite. Most astrophysicists consider this to be a natural explanation of the occurrence of satellites, rings, haloes, etc., of the planets. Sometimes the full tilting occurs in two steps as in the case of the earth or the planet Mars.

4. I have given the true origin of moon. Prof. Fred Singer had developed the theory of earth grabbing the moon from space, but in my view it was built on a scab released from the earth.

III. Materials Science and Operations Research

1. On joining Defence Scientific Research, it was natural to begin some work on operations research which seemed to be the main function of defence scientific work in India under the guidance of the Scientific Adviser Prof. D.S. Kothari. As a part of Naval research I calculated the optimum width of swept channel at Cochin and started

collating BT observations for use in anti-submarine search. A beginning in India was made on work on underwater sound, its propagation in the ocean. I applied fragmentation theory to understand that earth's continents did not appear as a result of single upheaval but as a result of separate causes like many volcanoes. I was concerned with the appearance of first sea wave and attached importance to gravity waves in the atmosphere. I developed the method of finding meaning in radar clutter which was-developed for the detection of distant horizons at sea.

I was concerned with administration for scientists and necessary ways to enthuse workers in a science laboratory using my long tenure as Director of the Defence Research Laboratory (Materials) at Kanpur. I was opposed to merit promotions, favouring only financial awards. The Kanpur laboratory demonstrated how good direction can produce research of merit from enthusiastic workers without high degrees but working for such degrees and attaining these. There was considerable work done there on degradation and preservation of materials, testing of materials, corrosion including underground corrosion and for designing and testing of fibre-polymer laminates. Most of this work was later published in my book *Science and Technology of Materials* in 1978 by Bombay Universal Corporation with a foreword by Prof. T.R. Seshadhri of the Delhi University. The book was widely used for engineering materials courses.

In two short appendices below are given my comments on important scientific issues before the country.

Appendix I

OCEAN SCIENCE WORK IN SOUTH ASIA

Ocean and Atmosphere are true international common. Only by international cooperation we may get to understand how nature controls weather and its changes. The ocean link between south-east Asian countries has been the most travelled since ancient times. India had established a lighthouse in far away Vietnam ! The sea fisheries are very important for the region. The subject has been discussed thoroughly in my book on *Cooperative Development of the Resources of the Sea* (Concept, Delhi 1989). The shallow water fishing craft depends only on storm signals for safety. Science could give them a workable instrument for instantaneous estimation of the biological content in the vertical column below their vessel, the principle of which has been given in my research paper on estimation of the biological content in the Journal of the Acoust. Soc. America in 1978, 9, pp. 618-620.

Appendix II

NUCLEAR POWER PLANTS

The world is short of power. Bhabha in India predicted the large scale use of nuclear energy in India since only other noteworthy resources: sunshine and winds are comparatively very costly. Nuclear power plants of about 250 MW are likely to be supplied by manufacturers in ready to start condition. The recent catastrophe in Japan has highlighted the necessity to build such plants to withstand damage in earthquake zones of known maximum intensity. India has been well aware of this warning. The first consideration would be to locate the site near the industrial spread where additional energy is not available from alternative sources. A primary concern would be the availability of large amount of cooling water. Foundation conditions have to be assessed carefully. Dispersion quality of wind or the flow of fluids at the site has to be adequate. Acceptable radiation dose is only 1.5 rem per year and the emergency dose is 25 rad. Monitoring is necessary to limit contamination by nuclides of Iodine (131), Caesium (137) and Strontium (90). Provision should exist for the emergency cooling of the core. Once through flow of at least 65000 cusecs is required to sustain the atomic power station. These notes are from notes prepared for lectures to army units while engaged on explaining nuclear energy and power to them.

Please see the list of important published papers on next page.

IMPORTANT RESEARCH PAPERS

Activity Coefficients of Electrolytes, 1982, *Proc. INSA*, Vol. 48, 584-588.
Atomic Explosions Inside Planets, 1989, *Proc. INSA,* Vol. 55, 630-638.
Conversion of Seismic Waves, 1959, *J.G.R.*, Vol. 64, p. 2032.

(With co-author K. Achyuthan) Periodicity in sea roughness and Origin of Microseism, 1958, *Nature*, Vol. 181, p. 646.

Earth's Innermost Core, (1989), *Proc. INSA,* Vol. 55, 101-109.

* Earth's Tilting and its Acquisition of Moon, sent for publication to *Ind. J. Phy.*, Kolkata-19 on March 30, 2011.

Evaluation of Crustal Characteristics from the Reverberation of Seismic Waves, 1958, *Proc. Roy. Soc.*, Vol. 256A, pp. 28-38.

* Helium inside Earth and Origin of Earth's Magnetic Dipole Field and its Reversals, sent for publication to Ind. National Sc. Acad., New Delhi-2 in March 2011.

* Internal Structure of the Earth and its Deep Core. Sent for Publication to *Proc. Ind. National Sc. Acad.* 110002 on 03/11.

Origin of Microseisms, 1960, *J. Geophys. Research*, 65, 1815-1818.

* Planetary Explosions (L), 2007, *Current Sc.*, Vol. 93, No. 2 (a reminder to readers sent for publication in March 2011)

*Significance of two atomic explosions in Earth. *Proc. INSA,* December 2011

Tilt of Planets, 1999, *Ind. J. Phy.*, 73 B, pp. 545-547. Coastal Floods and Vorticity IAPSO Publication No. 3 on "Present and Future of Oceanography". Area Search of a Moving Target, 1990 *Def. Sc. J.* New Delhi. Vol. 40, pp. 133-138.

Volume Scattering and Biological Content from Sea Bottom Echo Fluctuations 1978, *J. Acoust. Soc. America*, 63, 618-620.

(With co-author R.K. Tripathi) Prediction of Atmospheric Corrosion by Discriminate Analysis of local weather factors, 1972, British Corrosion Journal 7, pp. 212-215.

Note: The items above marked by * are going to be the resource papers of the new Earth Physics.

XIV

Life of Leisure in Delhi

The life at Delhi was very hectic from 1986 to 2011. This was the period when I quit working for salary from any other source besides the monthly pension and private rental income. I kept up my correspondence with other scientists and editors of research journals who were still wrapped up in ancient ideas about earth science. I would take up one of the pressing problems facing the country and try to write a book usually around some constructive approach. Apart from dilating on my work in earth physics, I kept publishing about one book per annum listed below:

Title	*Year*	*Publisher*
Materials Science and Technology	1978	Universal, Mumbai
Materials and Environment	1984	Inter Print, Delhi
Science and Technology in India's Transformation	1986	Concept, Delhi
Development of the Resources of the Sea	1989	Concept, Delhi
Conflicts and Co-existence	1991	Concept, Delhi
A Textbook of Geophysics	1997	Ashish Verma, Delhi
Foreign Policy of Co-existence	1997	Ashish Verma, Delhi
Glimpses of Indian History and Culture	2002	Bharatiya Vidya Bhavan
Glimpses of Indian History and Culture Hindi Translation	2003	Concept, Delhi
Religion and Philosophy for Modern Youth	2003	Concept, Delhi
Earth's Innermost Core	2004	Concept, Delhi
Bengal, The Unique State	2005	Concept, Delhi
Human Eternity: Stone Age to Mustopia	2006	Concept, Delhi
North East India	2007	Concept, Delhi
History of the Punjabees	2010	Concept, Delhi
Resurgent India (co-author M.S. Batra)	2011	Concept, Delhi
Earth – Moon sub system	2011	Zaheer Science Foundation

(A list of scientific papers has been given in chapter XIII).

I was severely shaken when my wife died after prolonged illness in 2009. She had loved life and was full of love for everyone. Her insights into human character and interrelationships had helped the even tenor of my life. We had three children and all adored her and have been eminently successful in shaping their careers. Eldest is my daughter Shashi Nanda Chawla, a topper of IIT, Delhi and now she has been very active as a dozent in Harvard museums and has talents in music and dance besides art, history, science and mathematics. My elder son Dinesh is in the top echelons of the Oil and Natural Gas Commission and the youngest Rajesh has toiled for becoming a successful surgeon and emergency doctor in a large regional Hospital in West Virginia, USA.

I am under obligation to dozens of relatives, friends and teachers. I hope they will accept my silent tribute. Still, I must record here my intense gratitude to my neighbours in Vasant Kunj for their great sympathy during my wife's illness, especially Mrs. Indra Kumar who throughout my wife's inability to walk around gave her full support during her daily programme of visits to shops, gardens, theatres, etc. and to Mrs. (Dr.) Somwal, our next door neighbour for readily giving any first aid and good medical advice.

I am maintaining my working life in the same busy rut as before with the support of my son Dinesh who lives in nearby Vasant Vihar. At the suggestion of my publisher, Shri Ashok Mittal, I have decided to bring up-to-date my autobiography first written in 1986 by adding few concluding pages. I have also a new close friend, my next door neighbour Shri Somwal who lost his wife about a year after I lost mine. We often call on each other without any formality and enjoy each other's company and discuss the news.

The highlights last year have been long deferred visits to Cambodia and Athens for paying my homage to Hindu temples and Indian culture of Angkar Wat and Cambodia. In Athens, I very much wished to see any memorablia of Socrates and Plato, but alas! The Greeks have forgotten them and are satisfied by all pervading Christian faith and churches. Athens is reduced to holiday resort for Europeans and is a most crowded dining hall with roads changed to arrays of dining tables. I visited the time honoured acropolis and temple of Athena and the Shrine at Olympus.

XV

New Mahayana and *Mustopia*

The abstract teaching of the Buddha placing the entire responsibility on an individual for own salvation through the noble eight-fold path appealing to any logical mind became the anchor of many peoples of the world, only through Mahayana which guaranteed also the place of faith and many godly helpers on the path to nirvana. The noble path and the yogic meditation and respectful involvement in worship and the acceptance of spiritual experiences of every kind including the single minded devotion of atheist reformers, and last but not the least the working for changes through non-violence alone, these are very much applicable now when the benefits of peaceful coexistence of diverse philosophies and practices are obvious. The alternative is the destruction through violent wars and struggles. Such destruction will be total with no survivors in the push button war of the future, the victors will have only the graves of people as their empire with practically total decimation of all. New ethics will have to come to terms with the limited resources of the earth and the preservation and upkeep of its environment. The scientific progress, it is hoped, will bring about miracles in human health and longevity, provide food and shelter at a reasonable level for a sustainable stable population. Even science may not increase living space in the biosphere which is of limited dimensions. Every-one will have to realize the equal importance of all human beings for the sustenance from this planet. A belief in the oneness of all creation need not be *via* a theistic belief in God, but could be from the logic of survival. New values of multi-religious beliefs and pragmatic non-violent political and economic thought will constitute the Mahayana of the post-industrial multi-polar world.

It is interesting that the philosophical thought started with the human being as the centre and was frankly atheist and humanist, e.g., Jainism. Soon, however, the people had the feeling of insufficiency without due recognition and charted ways to appease the gods or forces beyond human ken. Certain happenings were logical only if ascribed to a deity or destiny. Thus grew theism, faith and worship in pre-historic times. Due to lack of media assistance, differences, in "us and them", led to strife and struggle. Now and then, the Buddha, Marx, Roy, Nehru and many others harked back on humanism. Socialism and social justice must also come to terms with theism and religion for the stability and happiness of people. Gandhi's mahatmatics and Nehru's Fabian socialism combined to give meaning to India's secularism and mixed economy. India's secularism is such that even the fundamentalists of every religion are at home here; only they have to respect the other fundamentalists and find a way to enjoy each other's company.

We are naturally proud of our heritage from the pursuit of our religions. Could the Ellora caves, the giant statue of Gomteshwara and myriads of elaborate temples surpassing each other in beauty, grace and holiness or the Gothic cathedrals of Europe and the pyramids of Egypt, the stone-henge of England or the sun temples of the Aztecs, be built without the drive of religion. New Mahayana is emerging in India's secularism. Many art forms have developed in the world and each culture laid special emphasis on some particular form. The Hindus excelled in rhythm and music. Many civilizations and religions have contributed to sculpture and dance. Some have been profuse in painting. Islamic entry into India after crossing Iran and Afghanistan brought new skills in calligraphy and architecture. Ancient Egypt, Greece and Rome were more akin to India than to the modern west. The democracy practised in many ancient civilizations was only skin deep and the power pyramid rested on the backs of slaves. The women had usually an inferior status to men. There is continuity in the Indian tradition and in general the democracy was presided over by kings, but the rights of various professional castes were not to be taken lightly. The king was governing with the consent of the subjects who always had the right to select a better king. The modern Indian state has built on the hoary traditions and the latest documents on democracy and equality. The secular Indian state is totally committed to democracy and human rights. It is a pity that some of our contemporaries wish to see the reflection of violence, double talk and deceit of their own environment in the Indian mirror. The demolition of the fossil Babri Masjid had components of Hindu revivalism more than intolerance. There are thousands of mosques and Islamic religious and holy places spread throughout the length and breadth of the country. India being a land of the largest Muslim community in a multi-religious mass, the struggle if any is between the Pakistani version of exclusivism, and India's aim to surmount communalism by inculcation of proper values and the establishment of non-discriminatory laws and by assuring human rights to all its citizens including women and children. Far be it for me to gloss over many shortcomings of the Indian polity. Now and then rampant superstition surfaces in the form of human sacrifice, cruelty to women and children, but as Radhakrishnan has put it, culture is judged from the heights and not the pits that are yet to be smoothed.

India has been blessed with a basic philosophy most appropriate for world culture and world unity through the gospel of the middle path, humanism, mixed economy and social justice. We hold with Guru Govind Singh of the Sikhs that the cooperative thinking of many minds is the wisdom of God. Exclusivism and fanaticism is not specific to any religion. Tenaciously held non-religious beliefs can also lead to fanaticism. Jacobins and Stalinists are examples of non-religious fanaticism. Same is true of McCarthyism. Mobs that perpetrate riots and mad violence are temporarily swayed into fanaticism by demagogues often agitators or fanatic priests. Toleration of different views is essential for co-existence and the healthy state of the future world. The exclusiveness and the feeling that everything is known to a particular set of people and no new insight or interpretation can ever occur are childish. I once decided to go fishing on a Sunday, but I was assured by a neighbourhood child that I would catch no fish since he and his pa had caught all the fish on Saturday morning when they were at the lake.

In no other system is human, rather all life so central to the culture. The Hindu art of health care for longevity is receiving worldwide attention. Recently I invited a Philippine scientist, an official of the United Nations, who had expressed some interest, to observe our family worship on the festival of Diwali. I am still amused at his expression when he found us unabashedly worshipping the goddess of wealth and the god of auspicious beginnings and blessed completion i.e. the images of goddess Lakshmi and the elephant headed Ganesh placed in the same alcove. Even the major name of God with us is Satchidananda meaning Truth-Consciousness and Happiness. There is among the theists, a worldwide conjecture that consciousness is an objective reality and comes from without as soul when the human embryo is cast in the womb. Still how can human mind grasp an objective reality since any idea in one's mind will have to be subjective.

Indian folk art, possibly other folk arts too, are very much of the same family as modern art. They also go for the soul of objects as they hit the eye of the artist. Once I had the good fortune to talk to the most well known Indian artist Jaimini Roy who alas is no more now. I asked him to put the eyeballs, in the large eyes without the eyeballs in his famous painting of a dancer. He did so in my acquisition with great reluctance. I had explained that such eyes without eyeballs frightened me, but to him such eyes conveyed something artistic. Jaimini Roy had developed his style from the folk art of Bengal by his artistic genius. Indian music is highly developed and is now freely assimilating western perceptions. The English literature which has been a veritable Bible of the educated Indian for the last couple of centuries has made India the meeting place of the east and the west, just as in the times of the spread of the Buddhist Mahayaṇa, India was the Mecca of the entire east.

The progress lies in the automation especially of the common tasks of sanitation and landscaping so that the environment is preserved for the health and happiness of the people and the variety of life on the earth. In ancient times in the absence of sanitation technology, India devised the outcastes usually through punishment for social misdemeanours. A whole lot of people and their unfortunate descendants became low castes and outcastes of society little better than slaves. It is the development of sanitation technology that is freeing them from lowly tasks and allowing others to take up sanitation. Similarly the technical advances, the wheelbarrow, the power excavators, and the electric lifts have eased the back breaking jobs of yester year. The world is poised to welcome advances in weapons of mass destruction. The genii has to be put on leash possibly by strengthening the sensible trends in the United Nations. It will be a misfortune that the threat of nuclear holocaust or some serious nuclear plant accident turn humanity against scientific progress. Nehru was all for scientific method accepted by a populace, committed to scientific temper, that relies on human reason and accepts science and hopes to separate poison from nectar that accrues from the churning of nature by the continuous application of the intellect.

Ancient cultures: Indian, Chinese, Egyptian or Roman were in theory Puritanical, centred around the family and against excesses in sex, drugs, games of chance but were beset with these vices. The world is still struggling to master these. Certain nations have become corrupted by the mafias controlling these and of the wealth accruing to them from the ill gotten gains from drug abuse. India is targetted by the drug barons from both east (Burma/Thailand) and the west (Pakistan and international cartels) who would besides corrupting the Indian youths, use India as conduit to the west. India is at grips with this problem and invites the cooperation of the entire world in this as well as for combating terrorism which is being tried by certain states afflicted by the sickness of ambition and fanaticism. Indian culture upholds the family and the sanctity of marriage, only allowing divorce in rare cases.

Prudery in sex was never a Hindu virtue and they rarely suffer from guilt complex. Promiscuity historically has been seen in times of excessive prosperity as well as in days of excessive misery. The relief in the tenth century temples display in stone promiscuity for all to see. These were the days of excessive prosperity and piety when immense temples and structures were built. The global culture will find a middle way of plenty of legitimate sex.

The computers are becoming a store house of learning and information requiring only simple interrogation. When the blossoming of global culture proceeds, we would have to reinvent hieroglyphic form of language so that television screen and the printing media becomes intelligible to all irrespective of what way they speak; we would only be duplicating the feat that gave cultural unity to ancient China. The global culture being perfected in the east and the west and being implemented in India is the modern Mahayana of our type of secularism, tolerance, and democracy based on unity, nay, identity of all life. No one must be belittled to show honour to man or God.

Neither market nor socialist controls would be made a fetish at the cost of happiness of most people. Righteous pragmatism will be the paradigm of the new Mahayana arrived at through total system approach.

New Mahayana goes beyond tolerance and secularism to practically multi-religious essence. It is an outlook. A secular person recognizes merit irrespective of the religious label. New Mahayana outlook assumes the complexity of mind and accepts pluralism in beliefs and respects new symbols of cultural integration.

All places of worship are open to anyone who wishes to enter in a reverent attitude. School studies of ethics and morals can easily be inter-religious with illustrations freely chosen from the stories handed down in various communities. No one can be permitted to rail publicly at any worship. A person can have many levels of thinking in his brain and the human personality can harbour feelings of adoration and acceptance of many different concepts.

The new philosophy is against dictatorship of every kind, e.g., of capital, of labour, of clergy, or of demagogues, secularism, democracy and freedom exist together. Economic and social justice have to be striven for. Secularism can be strengthened by the reorientation of the training of priests and teachers, by overseeing the charities and by the management of religious institutions through authority of the Parliaments. Change and growth of values have to be managed to meet the world developments.

Only recently has the western mind grasped the lessons of science and technology and is applying them to social sciences. Everyone else has needs similar to one's own and our spiritual goals must also be the same. For an inter-religious society, any stamp of uniformity or private assurance of totality of knowledge is unthinkable. Secularism and new Mahayana are the important ingredients for the future mental progress. All religions favour virtue. Ethics and morals also develop with time. The stage has come for emphasis on many new secular virtues like patriotism, efficiency, creativity, and consistency between word and deed.

The global culture of tomorrow will be around multi-religious secularism and loving care for all mankind or around the new Mahayana. Heroes of the modern Mahayana will be Buddha, Ashoka, Socrates, Shankaracharya, Shakespeare, Akbar, Nanak, Tolstoy,

Gandhi, Martin Luther King, many Bodhisattvas including Ambedkar, human incarnations of God and gods, prophets, saints and martyrs. The Mahayana for the world in a nutshell is tolerance and sharing the feelings of pain and joy of others. Mahayana values have to be diligently propagated for the good of all. Value based education can be the key for handing over the elixir of life to the future generations.

High moral character, a loving nature full of sympathy and regard for others and a commitment to peaceful coexistence will lead to an inevitable utopia, i.e., a *mustopia* for whole mankind. This requires only a conscious effort of all nations to make the UN system of governance through independent and equal nations. Let us begin now.

Index